Six new AMERICAN HERITAGE JUNIOR LIBRARY *books are
published each year. Titles currently available are:*

TEXAS AND THE WAR WITH MEXICO

THE PILGRIMS AND PLYMOUTH COLONY

THE CALIFORNIA GOLD RUSH

PIRATES OF THE SPANISH MAIN

TRAPPERS AND MOUNTAIN MEN

MEN OF SCIENCE AND INVENTION

NAVAL BATTLES AND HEROES

THOMAS JEFFERSON AND HIS WORLD

DISCOVERERS OF THE NEW WORLD

RAILROADS IN THE DAYS OF STEAM

INDIANS OF THE PLAINS

THE STORY OF YANKEE WHALING

COVER: *The American troops in this painting are massed to attack the Mexicans holding
the fortified convent at Churubusco on August 20, 1847. When Churubusco fell to the
Americans the road to Mexico City, their chief objective, lay open to them. James
Walker, who painted this picture, was a British artist living in Mexico at the time of
the war; he joined the American army and served in many battles, including Churubusco.*

FRONT END SHEET: *This American cavalry charge probably took place either at the Battle
of Palo Alto (May 8, 1846) or at the Battle of Resaca de la Palma (May 9, 1846)—two
of the earliest battles of the Mexican War. The artist has mistakenly shown the cavalrymen charging in full-dress uniforms; actually, much simpler uniforms were worn in battle.*

HALF TITLE PAGE: *Davy Crockett (center), one of the Texans who attempted to hold the
Alamo in San Antonio against the Mexicans, is shown here as he falls, dying. The victorious troops of Mexican general Santa Anna are seen on the walls in the background.*

TITLE PAGE: The Battle of Buena Vista, *painted by Carl Nebel in 1847, shows General
Zachary Taylor mounted on his famous horse Old Whitey (center) directing the campaign
against Santa Anna's hard-fighting Mexican troops. This close battle, which was fought
on February 23 and February 24, 1847, ended in an important victory for the United
States and gave the United States Army virtual control of all of northern Mexico.*

BACK END SHEET: *This 1854 painting by James Walker shows American troops under the
command of General William Jenkins Worth breaking through the Mexican defenses at the
Gate of San Cosme, one of the principal entrances to Mexico City, on September 13, 1847.*

TEXAS AND THE WAR WITH MEXICO

ILLUSTRATED WITH PAINTINGS, PRINTS, DRAWINGS, MAPS, AND PHOTOGRAPHS OF THE PERIOD

WAR WITH MEXICO

BY THE EDITORS OF
AMERICAN HERITAGE
The Magazine of History

NARRATIVE BY
FAIRFAX DOWNEY

IN CONSULTATION WITH
PAUL M. ANGLE
Director, Chicago Historical Society

PUBLISHED BY
AMERICAN HERITAGE
PUBLISHING CO., INC.
NEW YORK

BOOK TRADE DISTRIBUTION BY
MEREDITH PRESS

INSTITUTIONAL DISTRIBUTION BY
HARPER & BROTHERS

Foreword

To most people of the United States the Mexican War is a dim, mildly disgraceful incident in the nation's past, hardly distinguishable from the War of 1812 or the war with the Seminole Indians. We fought with Mexico, whipped a general with a wooden leg, and grabbed some territory. Why bring it up well over a century later?

To that question there are several answers. We in the United States may have forgotten the Mexican War or stored it in the attic of our memories, but the Mexicans have not forgotten it. Proof of this statement is to be found in the veneration accorded by the Mexican people to *Los Niños,* the boy cadets who gave their lives in the defense of Chapultepec. As we revere the example of Nathan Hale —"I only regret that I have but one life to lose for my country"— so Mexico nurtures its own patriotism with equally heroic traditions.

We need not answer the question of responsibility for the war—was the United States the aggressor, or did Mexico provoke a tolerant nation beyond endurance?—to recognize the fact that through the war our country added enormously to its territory. An area including California, Nevada, Utah, and parts of Wyoming, Colorado, New Mexico, and Arizona came under the Stars and Stripes, and the status of Texas, annexed in 1845, was settled beyond doubt.

The Mexican War made Zachary Taylor President of the United States. It also gave invaluable experience to young American officers who would play leading parts in the Civil War—to Ulysses S. Grant, George H. Thomas, George G. Meade (among others) on the Union side; and to Robert E. Lee, Albert Sidney Johnston, Joseph E. Johnston, and Thomas J. "Stonewall" Jackson (again among others) in the Confederate forces.

All in all, the Mexican War deserves to be brought again to young readers, not to glorify the military might of the United States, but rather to broaden knowledge of a segment of American history the consequences of which reach to our own time.

PAUL M. ANGLE

FIRST EDITION

LIBRARY OF CONGRESS CATALOGUE CARD NUMBER: 61-16611

Sarah Borginnis (above) was famed for her bravery during the siege of Fort Brown in May, 1846. The fort, built on the Rio Grande opposite Matamoros, was commanded by Major Jacob Brown, who was killed in the siege.

Contents

10   EAGLE AND SERPENT

38   "REMEMBER THE ALAMO!"

58   LONE STAR JOINS THE UNION

70   "OLD ROUGH AND READY"

78   "MEXICO OR DEATH!"

86   WESTWARD TO CALIFORNIA

96   BUENA VISTA

104   FROM VERACRUZ TO CERRO GORDO

116   THE BATTLE OF CONTRERAS

124   CHURUBUSCO: PLACE OF THE WAR GOD

132   CHAPULTEPEC

150   PICTURE CREDITS

151   BIBLIOGRAPHY

152   INDEX

18

Entrada de
Cortes En Me
xico Por la Cal
sada de S Anto
nio Abad,

18

Eagle and Serpent

In the spring of 1846, bugles in the United States army camp near the Mexican border sounded "Boots and Saddles" and "To Horse."

Old Whitey, General Zachary Taylor's charger, stood quietly while the commander mounted. The horse, named for the color of his hide, would behave as calmly and steadily in battle under shell fire and hail of bullets. Now he stepped out, as fifes and drums joined the bugles. With dragoons and Texas Rangers scouting ahead, the army marched to war.

The story of the war with Mexico can well begin with Old Whitey because horses were closely connected with the history of Mexico ever since they had been introduced there, and they played a highly important part all through the conflict of 1846-48 and long before it.

Old Whitey was a Mexican horse, descended from Barbs and Arabians, the splendid steeds brought by the Spaniards who invaded Mexico under Cortés in 1519-21 and conquered the Aztec Indian empire of Montezuma.

The device above, dominated by an eagle grasping a serpent, is taken from a Mexican battle flag captured by American troops during the Mexican War. The eagle and serpent design—which became part of the Mexican coat of arms when independence from Spain was declared—is an Aztec symbol; the eagle represents Huitzilopochtli, the special god and patron of the Aztecs; he is grasping a fire serpent, a ray of the sun. The 1698 Spanish painting at left shows the entry of Hernando Cortés and his Spanish army into Mexico City in 1521, after the Aztecs' defeat.

For nearly three centuries after Montezuma's city had been stormed and gutted of its treasures, Mexico was held as a province, firm in the grasp of Spain.

The horses of the conquistadors carried the banner of Spain north and west, beyond the horizon, in an unending search for riches. Somewhere ahead, the Spaniards had heard, lay the Seven Cities of Cibola, paved with gold; shining Quivira; glittering Eldorado.

Where the sword went the cross went, too. The armored conquistadors never found their cities of gold, but the priests in brown robes with crosses swinging from their waists located the kind of treasure they were seeking—heathens to be converted to Christianity.

In the seventeenth century New Mexico was colonized; in the eighteenth California was settled. When they rode north from Mexico City in the early 1700's, the Spanish invaded the Tejas Indians' land, later to be known as Texas. Over that ground five flags would float after Spain's: the eagle emblem of Mexico, the golden Lilies of France, the Lone Star of Texas, the Stars and Stripes, the Stars and Bars of the Confederate States, and finally, the Star-Spangled Banner once more.

All the vast lands of the Missouri Valley—the territory called Louisiana—shifted back and forth between Spain and France before they were bought by the United States. Claimed by the Frenchman La Salle in 1682,

Louisiana was held by France for eighty years. But when in 1763 England won Canada in the French and Indian War, France (to keep Louisiana from the southward-reaching grasp of Britain) suddenly traded that great expanse to Spain in exchange for a single Mediterranean island. Then, in 1800, the powerful France of Napoleon Bonaparte wrested back Louisiana from the Spaniards. But Napoleon did not hold it long. At death grips with the British in a European war, he knew he could not defend his big possession across the sea. So he sold it to the United States for $15,000,000—about three cents an acre. The Louisiana Purchase, that splendid bargain, was made in 1803 during the administration of President Jefferson.

Elsewhere the mighty empire of Spain in the New World did not remain unchallenged. Russian fur traders pushed southward along the Pacific Coast from Sitka, Alaska, and threatened California. Americans from the new nation born in 1776 began to settle on the soil of Mexico—in Texas, in the Southwest, and in California. Spain held Florida until 1819; then sold it to the United States for $5,000,000. As the nineteenth century advanced, American pressure on the realms of Spain and Mexico increased.

For the Spaniards and the Mexicans, after wresting wide western territories from the Indians, had turned those lands into tempting prizes.

From Mexico and Texas and on to California the friars established mis-

The Italian artist Claudio Linati made these drawings of a Mexican monk (right) and an Apache Indian cacique (chief) during a visit to Mexico in 1825-26. Monks like this one worked for the conversion of the Indians to Christianity and fought the encomienda *system*, *established in the sixteenth century, which gave the* encomienderos *(landowners) the right to enslave the Indians living on their land. The system was abolished in the 1700's.*

sions that held the empire together as links form a chain. And the settlers established estates, the haciendas and ranchos on whose produce the empire lived. There, in those estates and cattle ranches, lay the true wealth of the land—not in gold and gems but in cattle and wheat and maize, in flax and fruit and furs.

Gardens bloomed with flowers and fruit trees. Crops were harvested from furrowed fields. Dashing vaqueros, the first cowboys of North America, galloped through plains and valleys to round up the longhorn cattle.

It was a fascinating civilization that grew up in Mexico, built on the ruins of the Aztec empire and that of the Mayan Indians before them. As much as the soldiers and the settlers and the governors, it was the friars of the monastic orders, the brown-robed Franciscans and the black-robed Jesuits, who made New Spain thrive.

They were selfless and faithful men, those friars, and brave ones. Some died as martyrs, slain by Indian arrows. Under the leadership of such great missionaries as Fra Junípero Serra and Fra Bartolomé de las Casas they carried on their good works wherever the banners of Spain or Mexico flew. They converted the friendlier Indians and taught them to build and plant and tend herds and flocks.

Through many years the padres fought for the rights of the Indians as human beings. Really they were held in slavery, though the Spaniards called it "personal service." Sometimes treat-

ment was kind. Too often it was harsh and cruel, especially at the mines and pearl fisheries. Despite the efforts of the missionaries, it was not until 1794 that the king's decree granted the Indians freedom, and then it was frequently only so in name. Spain's empire in the New World depended on slavery as definitely as did plantations of the American South.

At the opposite end of Mexico's class structure were the *Gachupines* (those who had been born in Spain) and *criollos* or Creoles (those born in the New World), men and women who proudly cherished their European ancestry. There was a fierce resentment, however, between these two privileged classes. The Spanish-born *Gachupines*, not wanting political power ever to get into the hands of native-born Mexicans (even rich and aristocratic Mexicans), forbade the Creoles to hold key Church or government offices in Mexico. These positions had to be held by the *Gachupines*, who were assumed to be Mexico's most loyal subjects of the Spanish Crown. The discontent of many Creoles with this system was one day to contribute to the end of Spanish rule in Mexico. Next to the two antagonistic ruling classes ranked the mestizos, half-breeds of Spanish and Indian parentage. They, like the pure-bloods, lorded it over Indians and Negroes and mixtures of those two races called *zambos*.

For the Spanish and Mexican ruling classes—the *gentes de razón* (the people of reason), as they termed them-

The mission of San José (above) in San Antonio, Texas, was founded in 1720. San José, which was built in typical Spanish colonial style, was one of a great system of missions that Spain set up in her New World colonies to help bring Christianity to the Indians.

OVERLEAF: *Much of the land of Mexico—both during and after Spanish rule—was controlled by the owners of haciendas (estates) like the one shown in this eighteenth-century painting. The owner of the estate lived in the house behind the high stone wall at center.*

selves—it was often a delightful life. The one-story adobe houses of their haciendas contained rooms opening on a charming inner patio, shaded by cottonwood trees. Besides the bedrooms and a little chapel, storerooms, and servants' quarters, there was a big hall or *sala* for dances and other parties. Its walls were hung with silks from China, brought by the Spanish galleons from the Philippines. Everybody ate in the kitchen where Indian women cooked delicious food served on silver plates: that tasty shellfish abalone, if the hacienda was near the Pacific; roast stuffed pigeon and turkey, or an *olla* or stew of well-spiced beef or mutton with red beans, peas, and greens; tamales and enchiladas; wines from the vineyards of the missions, and hot chocolate. Near the house there would be the blacksmith shop and the stables, with ready-saddled horses tethered to a hitching rail, for almost everyone in Spanish Mexico rode horses, mules, or burros.

Boys often learned to ride at the age of four, when they were lifted onto the backs of cow ponies. Since their legs were too short to grip a saddle, vaqueros on either side steadied them as they started off. Women and girls also became expert horsewomen. In California they rode and dressed like vaqueros. Broad-brimmed, low-crowned hats, secured by thongs under their chins, sat at rakish angles on the black silk handkerchiefs around their heads. Their hair was braided and tied with ribbons at the back like men's, also worn long. Jackets were brightly colored and embroidered. From wide leather belts hung buckskin *armitas* or chaps, which protected their legs from cactus thorns. Spurs on their boots were silver with long rowels, and a dagger in a scabbard was strapped to their right leg. These girls broke colts and took part in the roundups, roping cattle along with the men.

What gay evenings there were when the people of the haciendas met to dance a fandango. Fiddles, guitars, and flutes struck up a lively tune. Graceful *señoritas* swept into the *sala,* that spacious hall. Over their flowing tresses black lace mantillas were draped from high, carved, tortoise-shell combs. Strings of lustrous pearls shone on slender necks. Embroidered jackets fitted closely above the wide flair of skirts of flowered silk. Partnering them were *caballeros* in black velvet with brightly colored *serapes* or scarves swinging from shoulders.

For some of the haciendas, remote from towns or forts, there were times of deadly peril. *"Indios!"* warned a shout. A dust cloud had been sighted, stirred by galloping hoofs of the ponies of Apache, Comanche, or Kiowa raiders. It sped in fast. The chapel bell tolled a frantic alarm. Men ran from their work in the fields and children from their play. Doors of the big house clanged closed behind them—behind all who had not been too far away to reach safety. The crumpled bodies of those unlucky ones lay on the ground,

Bernardo de Gálvez (above)—who was Spanish governor of Louisiana during the American Revolution—did everything he could to assist the thirteen colonies in winning independence from England. The friendly relationship between the United States and its Mexican neighbors brought about by Gálvez and others lasted until the 1830's; it was then that Mexico began to fear the fast-growing United States.

pierced by lances, riddled with arrows, and scalped.

Defenders behind the parapets of the roof poked the barrels of their muskets through the gutter spouts. There were sharp reports and spurts of flame, and some of the raiders toppled from their ponies. Others raced forward on foot behind volleys of answering shots and flights of arrows. Sometimes they broke in or crawled through the water ditch to massacre every man, woman, and child and leave the house a smoking ruin. But usually they were beaten off and dashed back to the mountains after burning crops and driving off horses and cows.

From Texas to California the white men struck back, holding the land they had conquered. Musketeers and dragoons and bands of armed settlers marched against the hostile tribes. The red men, defeated in pitched battles, were driven deeper into the mountains and the plains.

Some Mexican cavalrymen, when

they fought Indians, were armed only with riatas, or lariats, preferring them to carbine or lance. As sure or surer than shot or thrust were the long, deadly throws that noosed and choked enemy bowmen. Some American soldiers in the war to come would meet such a fate when Mexican ropes circled their necks or bound their arms helplessly to their sides.

Mexicans, fighting Indians since the days of Cortés and Coronado, had to be a warlike people to keep the ground they had won. They must also stave off the French threat from Louisiana. While they fought in the New World, their mother country, Spain, engaged in wars with France and England in Europe and at sea. From the beginning there was no lack of conflict.

But friendly relations increased between Mexico and the English colonies of North America. That was especially true after Virginians, the men of Massachusetts, and the rest rebelled and declared their independence in 1776. Mexicans sympathized with them, since Spain and France were allied against England. During the Revolution, the Spanish governor of Louisiana, Bernardo de Gálvez, helped the Americans in every possible way. He opened New Orleans to them and held British frigates in port, keeping them out of action. When Spain went to war with England in 1779, Gálvez captured British forts on the Gulf of Mexico. A town in Texas later was named Galveston in his honor.

Few Mexicans or Americans real-

ized, at the time of the American Revolution, how soon after 1776 a revolutionary movement would sweep Mexico. In 1808 Napoleon Bonaparte, the emperor of France, deposed the rightful king of Spain, Ferdinand VII, and placed his own brother, Joseph Bonaparte, on the Spanish throne. When the Mexicans received news that their king had been deposed—for Ferdinand VII was as much their king as he was king of the Spaniards—many

Mexicans considered Joseph Bonaparte's government to be illegal.

It was in 1808, therefore, that the first strong feeling of independence began to develop in the Mexican people—and in most of the countries of South America. And this feeling continued to grow—once aroused—even though Joseph Bonaparte was deposed in 1813 and Ferdinand VII was restored in 1814.

On September 16, 1810, the first

The picture below shows a busy plaza in Mexico City around 1850. The plaza looks much as it would have looked in the days before Mexico's independence from Spain. Mexico kept its traditional way of life—with the strict class system established by Spain—virtually unchanged until the twentieth century. The Creole ladies and gentlemen shown here are chatting near their waiting carriages. The pack mules in the plaza are driven by peasants bringing goods to market.

open rebellion of Mexicans against Spanish rule began in the little town of Dolores. The movement was led by a Mexican Creole priest, Father Hidalgo y Costilla. Assisted by two other revolutionary leaders, Father Hidalgo recruited a small army of Creoles and mestizos and took the Mexican cities of Guanajuato and Guadalajara from the Spanish forces. Then, with an army of about 80,000 men, he marched on Mexico City. Although Hidalgo's army had some preliminary victories, it was defeated by a Spanish army on November 6, 1810. Early in 1811, after more defeats at the hands of the Spanish, Father Hidalgo was captured and later shot, with the men who had supported him. Despite the ultimate failure of his mission, Father Hidalgo was the first hero of the Mexican Revolution, and the day of the uprising he led in Dolores—

September 16, 1810—is still celebrated as Mexican Independence Day.

After Father Hidalgo's first move to start the Mexican Revolution, other Mexican leaders began to appear. Father Morelos, a mestizo priest who had served in Hidalgo's revolutionary army, took over leadership of the revolution after Hidalgo's execution. Morelos, however, had the *Gachupines*, the conservative Mexicans, and the Mexican monarchists against him. The rich Creoles and *Gachupines* had never intended to support a revolution which might hurt their privileged position, and the Morelos revolution was rapidly taking on the look of popular uprising, supported by Indians and mestizos. Morelos suffered a series of defeats and in 1815 was captured by the Spanish forces and—suffering the same fate as Father Hidalgo—was executed by a firing squad.

Because of the discoveries of her explorers of the fifteenth, sixteenth, and seventeenth centuries, Spain claimed much of the eastern United States of today, as well as controlling the areas shown at right. Spain's primary interest, however, was in her Central and South American empire; because of this, many Spanish claims in North America were not supported by troops and outposts. For over one hundred years—beginning in 1670—England and Spain contested control of the coastal area from Charleston, South Carolina, to St. Augustine, Florida. When Spain lost the Louisiana Territory, she lost control of Mississippi River traffic. Spain took little interest in settling Texas or California until the 1700's; settlement of Texas began in 1718 because Spain feared French interest in it; settlement of California began in 1769 because Spain feared the claims of both Russia and England on the territory.

DISPUTED BY
SPAIN, RUSSIA
& ENGLAND

CEDED BY U.S.

BRITISH-AMERICAN TREATY LINE OF 1818

CEDED TO U.S.

CANADA

SPANISH-AMERICAN TREATY LINE OF 1819

42ND PARALLEL

LOUISIANA

TERRITORY

(SPANISH HELD 1763-1800)

NATURAL BOUNDARY OF LOUISIANA

UNITED STATES

OF

AMERICA

Francisco

nterey

Arkansas R.

Missouri R.

les

San Diego

Santa Fe

NATURAL BOUNDARY OF LOUISIANA

Red R.

Mississippi R.

El Paso
del Norte

Río Grande

San
Antonio

SPANISH-AMERICAN
TREATY LINE OF 1819

B. New
Orleans

FLORIDA

ATLANTIC OCEAN

BAHAMAS

VICEROYALTY

OF

NEW SPAIN

GULF OF
MEXICO

CUBA

FIC OCEAN

JAMAICA

Mexico
City

N

EXTENT OF
SPANISH TERRITORY
IN NORTH AMERICA
CIRCA 1790

0   100   200   300 Miles
Scale

23

Negro Boatman

Vendor

Creole Landowner

Creole Lady

Mexican Creoles (people of Spanish descent born in Mexico) like the couple in the Linati drawing above became the ruling class of Mexico when independence from Spain was declared in
1821. The key posts in the government, the Church, and the army had formerly been held by
Spanish-born Gachupines. The drawings of Mexicans on the opposite page are also by Linati.
The vendor is probably a mestizo (a person of mixed Spanish and Indian blood); the Creole lady,
as part of the fulfillment of a religious vow, has dressed her son as a Franciscan monk or friar.

In 1820 revolution broke out again. That year word reached Mexico of an uprising against Ferdinand VII in Spain, and the Mexican ruling class decided that the only way to protect itself and preserve its way of life was to revive the revolution Father Hidalgo had started and to seize control of it.

The spokesman for the new conservative revolutionary movement in Mexico was Agustín Iturbide, a former Spanish army officer who had fought against Father Morelos. Iturbide and his followers wanted an independent Mexican monarchy as severe and autocratic as Spain's monarchy had been before the Napoleonic Wars. In 1821, most members of the ruling classes in Mexico agreed on the Plan de Iguala, which was both a declaration of independence from Spain and a plan for the new monarchy of Mexico. In July, 1821, a newly appointed Spanish viceroy of Mexico, Juan O'Donojú, arrived at Veracruz. He was informed by the Mexican authorities that he would not be allowed to proceed to Mexico City and take office because Mexico was independent of Spain. Since the revolutionaries had established their control over the army, O'Donojú had no choice but to recognize Mexican independence—which he did by signing the Treaty of Córdoba. On September 27, 1821, Iturbide entered Mexico City as a revolutionary hero and as the future emperor of Mexico.

Mexico's history as an independent nation was not to be calm. Iturbide

The picture at right shows the capture of Father Hidalgo—on horseback in front—by Spanish troops on March 21, 1811. Mexico's first revolutionary leader was found and arrested on a road in the state of Chihuahua.

In the scene below, Father Hidalgo, shown kneeling at right with a cross in his hand, and another revolutionary leader are executed by a firing squad on July 31, 1811. In the rear, more of Hidalgo's followers are being put to death.

was crowned emperor of Mexico on July 21, 1822—with the support of the army. But he was not a popular ruler and was deposed in 1823 and executed in 1824 when he again tried to seize control of the government by force.

On October 4, 1824, a new constitution was proclaimed, by which Mexico became a republic. Later that year the nation elected its first president—a man who called himself Guadalupe Victoria (Our Lady of Guadalupe Triumphant)—although his name was actually Manuel Félix Fernández—because Guadalupe Victoria had been the motto and battle cry of the revolutionary armies of Father Hidalgo and Father Morelos in which he had served. Our Lady of Guadalupe was the patron saint of Mexico and was, therefore, honored by all classes of Mexican society.

The government that Guadalupe Victoria headed remained in power until 1829. The elections for a new president, held in 1828, saw Manuel Gómez Pedraza and Vicente Guerrero as the chief contenders for office. Pedraza won the election, but Guerrero soon

The inn above left was painted by the Mexican artist Augustín Arrieta in the 1840's. Inns were very popular gathering places for Mexican workmen, merchants, and craftsmen.

The Mexican upper class could entertain as elegantly as the Spanish aristocracy. The scene at left shows a banquet given in honor of a Mexican government official in 1844.

pushed Pedraza aside and had himself inaugurated as president of Mexico on April 1, 1829.

Guerrero's term of office was to be short and hectic. On August 18, 1829, an invasion force of Spaniards from Cuba landed at Tampico and took it from the Mexican garrison in a last effort to recapture Mexico.

Antonio López de Santa Anna, who had long been active in Mexican politics and had been a soldier in both the Spanish and Mexican armies, led the Mexican force sent to Tampico to drive out the Spanish. His army was victorious on September 11, 1829, when the Spanish were finally forced to surrender the city. Because of his impressive military success, within a very short time Santa Anna became a Mexican national hero.

On September 15, 1829, Guerrero's administration made more Mexican history by announcing the abolition of slavery in Mexico—making Mexico one of the first countries in the Western Hemisphere to take this step. Although it is quite possible that the Guerrero administration sincerely disapproved of slavery, the action they took in freeing the slaves of Mexico and outlawing slavery in their country was specifically directed at the slave-owning Americans who had settled, by this time, in the northern province of the state of Coahuila which was known as Texas. For these Americans were the only sizable group of slaveowners in Mexico.

The hero of Tampico, Santa Anna,

Guadalupe Victoria (above) was inaugurated in the fall of 1824 as Mexico's first elected president. His government succeeded Iturbide's.

Augustín Iturbide (left) posed for this portrait in 1822, after becoming Emperor Augustín I, the first ruler of an independent Mexico.

was unwilling to allow the Guerrero administration to become too popular, however, for he had always had personal political ambitions. In an undercover attempt to break Guerrero's power, Santa Anna, in December, 1829, helped Guerrero's vice president, Anastasio Bustamante, stage a revolution against Guerrero. Early in 1830, Bustamante became president. Santa Anna, however, was still not satisfied with the Mexican government and would not be content until he headed it himself. In an attempt to bring himself closer to the presidency, Santa Anna engineered, in 1832, a revolution against Bustamante. The revolution was successful, and Pedraza — who was supported by Santa Anna—finished serving the final three months of the term in office he should have had to begin with. For it was Pedraza, the legally elected president of Mexico in 1829, from whom Guerrero had originally stolen the presidency.

In 1833 Santa Anna ran for president and won the election. The following year he dissolved the Congress, established himself as dictator of Mexico, and for the next twenty years dominated the politics of his country.

One of Santa Anna's first major acts as dictator of Mexico was to send his

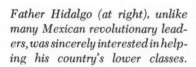

Father Hidalgo (at right), unlike many Mexican revolutionary leaders, was sincerely interested in helping his country's lower classes.

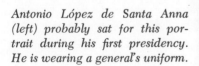

Antonio López de Santa Anna (left) probably sat for this portrait during his first presidency. He is wearing a general's uniform.

31

brother-in-law, General Martín Cos, to Texas, for reasons which will be discussed in the following chapter. As soon as the Texans learned of this move, they decided to resist General Cos. Fighting began in Gonzales and in San Antonio late in 1835.

Although Santa Anna knew that he would have a difficult time subduing the Texans, he went on with his establishment of a strong, centralized, and dictatorial government in Mexico City. On December 30, 1836, Santa Anna's new constitution—called the *Siete Leyes* (Seven Laws)—was proclaimed. This constitution broke the power of the traditional Mexican states. The states could no longer elect their own officials but would be supplied with officials appointed by Santa Anna's

Father José María Morelos became a Mexican revolutionary leader after the death of Father Hidalgo. On November 15, 1815—after launching many well-planned and successful military campaigns—Morelos was captured by the Spanish (left); he appears at center. On December 22, 1815, at a spot outside Mexico City, the kneeling Morelos (below left) was put to death by a firing squad. The order for his execution was given by Félix María Calleja del Rey, the Spanish commander in charge of crushing revolutionary activity in Mexico.

This portrait of Father Morelos was painted by an Indian artist, probably in 1814, the year before his death. He is wearing the uniform of a general; the only reminder of his priesthood is the gold cross on his tunic.

33

At dawn on May 19, 1822, Augustín Iturbide—shown standing in the center of the balcony at right—was proclaimed emperor of Mexico. This colorful scene in Mexico City came after a heated debate

...tween those Mexican leaders who wanted a republic and those who wanted a monarchy; the monarchists won after receiving the support of the army. Iturbide was crowned on July 21, 1822.

*These four American Presidents played im-
portant roles in the history of Texas and in
the relations of the United States and Mexico. In 1827 Adams offered to buy Texas
from Mexico for $1,000,000 and was refused;
in 1829 Jackson offered $5,000,000 and was
also refused. Texas became an independent
republic in 1836, and Jackson, afraid of pro-
voking Mexico into a war, delayed recognizing the new nation as long as possible. Finally, as the last act of his administration,
he granted recognition in 1837, making the
United States the first nation to do so. Van
Buren was also cautious about Texas. He
did not permit annexation of Texas by the
United States in his administration because
he feared a split in Congress over the admission of what would surely be a slave state. As
the final act of his administration, President Tyler signed the bill admitting Texas
to the Union and placing the United States
on the brink of open conflict with Mexico.*

central government in Mexico City. In
fact all of Mexico was to be controlled
by Santa Anna's government, which
represented the most conservative ele-
ments in Mexico—the Church and the
most powerful landowners. Needless
to say, the great mass of the Mexican
people did not benefit in any material
way from Mexico's early revolutions—
or even from independence from
Spain. For of Mexico's seven million
citizens, only ten per cent were considered eligible to play any part at all
in the government of their country.
The Creoles made up this ten per cent,
while the rest of Mexico's population
was made up of poor and ignorant Indians and Negroes and of mixtures of

*John Quincy Adams
President: 1825-29*

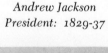

*Andrew Jackson
President: 1829-37*

the races. This was basically the situation that had existed under Spanish rule, and it would not change until late in the nineteenth century. Until that time, Mexico's revolutions were all Creole struggles to gain governmental power and control.

During this period of turmoil in Mexico, up until 1830, *Yanqui* settlers had been welcome in Texas, the Southwest, and California. There was plenty of land, and these men from the north were hard workers. Their ranches and fields had flourished, and they had paid taxes to the Mexican treasury. So long as they had been treated fairly they had been content.

But when the banner of Spain lowered forever, the flag of Mexico—displaying an eagle clutching a serpent in his talons upon its white stripe, bordered with red and green stripes— would become a symbol to the *Yanquis* of a sterner and even menacing Mexico. It fluttered from staffs in the plazas of such Texas towns as La Bahia, or Goliad, and of San Antonio. Its shadow fell on their strong-walled mission churches — Goliad's Espiritu Santo and San Antonio's Alamo. One of the flag's stripes would soon seem to glow blood-red in the sunlight. The time was coming when those churches would give American settlers in Texas two battle cries: "Remember Goliad!" and "Remember the Alamo!"

Martin Van Buren
President: 1837-41

John Tyler
President: 1841-45

37

"Remember the Alamo!"

Nobody really knew where "P. H. N. Tut, Baron de Bastrop" had come from. But by 1820, as a Texas *empresario* (as the Spanish termed their government land agents) he was a close friend of Antonio Martínez, the Spanish governor of the state of Coahuila. Baron de Bastrop was a close enough friend of Martínez' to persuade him to reconsider and change his mind after he had once refused to grant land to Moses Austin, land speculator of Connecticut, Virginia, Missouri, and Arkansas — for Martínez later granted Austin enough land to establish an Anglo-American colony on Texas' rough, wild prairies.

Moses Austin had been pushed across the border from Missouri by the financial panic of 1819, which had stunned the southwestern United States. He had been a banker, mine owner, and slaveholder. Since the Missouri Compromise of 1820 had closed land north of the 36°30′ parallel to slavery, Moses Austin saw in Texas a chance for farmers and cotton planters to settle on its spacious lands. His deci-

The picture at left shows Stephen F. Austin (center) in his cabin at San Felipe de Austin in 1824. Baron de Bastrop, who had helped Austin's father, is seated at far left.

sion to go to Texas was to end in the creation of a short-term nation, in the making of a President of the United States, and it almost caused the Civil War to begin a generation sooner than it did. His plans were large-scale, but on the way back from Texas, he died.

There was nobody to take over his colony but his son Stephen, who had already, at twenty-seven—after serving in the Missouri Territorial Legislature at the time when Missouri was brought into the Union as a slave state—settled in elegant, civilized New Orleans to study law.

Stephen Austin was a small man, gentle in manner, always neatly dressed. Nobody would ever have singled him out as the leader of American pioneers in the wild, rough Mexican province of Texas. Choosing rich land between the Colorado and Brazos rivers for his promised grant, he rode into Texas with a vanguard of three hundred families in 1821.

Austin accepted his inheritance with some reluctance. He would never have undertaken the venture except as a son's duty. On several occasions he traveled to Mexico City in an attempt to establish his claims, and finally, in 1823, in the midst of Mexico's political upsets, he succeeded. His success was

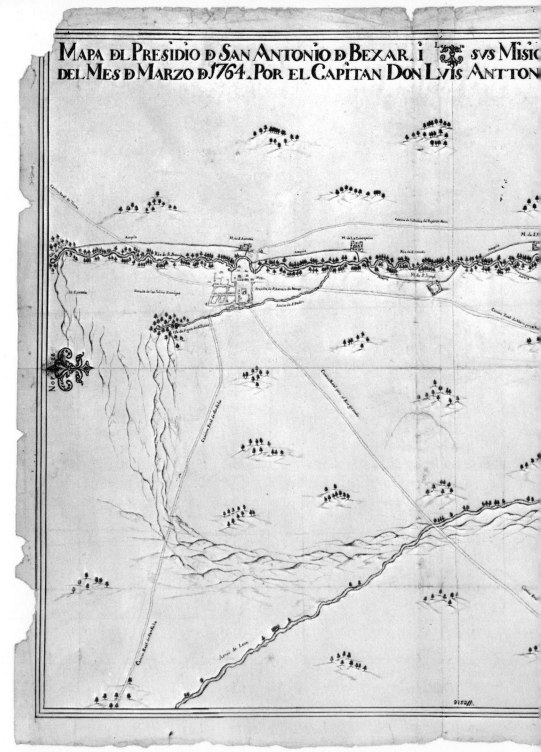

In the 1764 map above, the settlement and presidio (fort) of San Antonio de Bexar are shown (upper left) on the San Antonio River at the site of present-day San Antonio, Texas; the settlement was established by the Spanish in 1718. The Mission of San Antonio de Valero—better known later as the Alamo—is seen directly across the San Antonio River from the settlement.

even more surprising in view of Mexico's growing fear of an always encroaching United States. The Louisiana Purchase in 1803 had brought the American border to the province of Texas. And in 1819 the United States had forced Spain to sell Florida. Toward Austin's lands in Texas covered wagons pulled by ox teams rolled into the Southwest.

Each family was given at least 640 acres at low cost and with freedom from taxation for six years. They were willing to turn their backs on the United States, to pledge allegiance to Mexico, and to adopt her Roman Catholic religion, as they were required to do, in return for the bright opportunity that lay ahead.

By 1830, Austin had settled two of the colonists' most pressing problems.

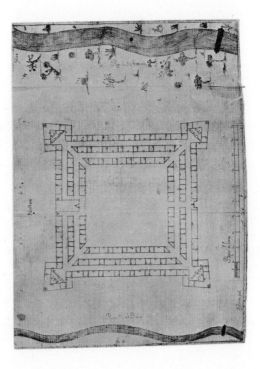

The drawing at right of the fortifications of the presidio of San Antonio de Bexar—a typical eighteenth-century fort—was made in 1722, four years after its founding.

They were to be allowed to keep slaves in Texas (even though no other portions of Mexico held slaves after 1829). Austin also arranged for Texans to be protected by the Mexican government from suits to collect debts they had contracted in the United States before their immigration to Texas. All over the depressed South, signs were to appear on the doors of bankrupt homes— "Gone to Texas."

These colonists from the United States would help the country prosper. They would fight off raiding Indians. It was believed that they would mingle with the native Mexicans and be absorbed into the nation. The first American settlement in Texas was made in good faith on both sides.

Austin and many of his people long kept that faith. But there were firebrands among them, restless, hot-tempered men ready to start trouble for any government unless it was strong and wise. And they soon found chances to stir up trouble under the uncertain, changeable Mexican rule.

Mexican authorities grew worried that too many Americans were coming to their country. An estimated thirty thousand settlers had poured into Texas in the decade after Austin established his colony. Though they were naturalized Mexican citizens, they were still foreigners, speaking a different language. The Mexican Congress, under the urging of President Bustamante, passed severe laws against the immigration of more colonists in 1830. Trade with the United States was severely restricted. The border was to be closed to new colonists, but the long border between Louisiana and Texas could not be patrolled. Bustamante sent Mier y Teran with troops to enforce obedience, a few soldiers to stop a flood. It is said that he committed suicide, driven to despair by his failure to stop further colonization.

Texas hummed like a nest of angry hornets. American settlers were put into prison, often for trifling offenses. Among those that were imprisoned was Stephen Austin.

Sam Houston

Erastus Smith

Benjamin Milam

In July, 1833, he had arrived in Mexico City to plead the càuse of the colonists he led. They wanted to separate from the state of Coahuila and obtain full Mexican statehood for Texas, exercise control over their own affairs, have a capital more convenient to the colony, and be spared the growing nuisance of arrogant Mexican officials.

Austin presented their case, but the Mexican rulers would not listen to him. He started home, but was arrested at Saltillo on January 3, 1834, after a letter of his had been intercepted. In it he had—in defiance of Mexican law—advised the Texans to establish themselves as a separate state of Mexico if his appeal failed. Charged with treason, he was jailed for eighteen months.

Texans gathered in protest meetings. The answer of the Mexican Congress was to order them to be disarmed, and more soldiers were sent.

Austin continued to try to persuade Texans to keep the peace when he was released from prison. But by this time almost absolute power in Mexico had been·seized by Antonio López de Santa Anna, who had been elected president of Mexico in late 1833. He envied the career of Bonaparte and liked to be called "the Napoleon of the West." In gorgeous, bemedalled uniform he bestrode a handsome charger. His saddle was stamped with gold, its horn in the shape of an eagle head. His was a quick mind and an imperious will.

In the fall of 1835, Santa Anna sent more Mexican troops into Texas under General Martín Cos, his brother-in-law, to patrol the border and to enforce the immigration laws. Austin, who had been released from prison and had returned to Texas on September 1, announced on September 21 that Cos had landed at Copano. A cordon began to close around the settlements, and the towns were occupied. Mexico now considered that the Texans were on the verge of rebellion against their adopted country and that there was no way to deal with them now but to overawe them by military force. Tex-

William Travis

These four men had one important thing in common: a love of Texas and a willingness to fight for its independence. All of them were experienced fighters; Sam Houston, however, was the most experienced soldier of them all. He had served in the War of 1812 and had been a general in the Tennessee militia. Smith—nicknamed "Deaf"—was a famous scout and knew well the land for which they were to fight. Ben Milam also knew Texas; he was one of the party that made the first ascent of the Red River by steamboat in 1831. Travis, who it is thought came to Texas after killing a man in a fight over a girl, was an avid reader of Sir Walter Scott's adventure novels about knights and heroes, and would one day become a hero himself.

As early as the spring of 1829 Sam Houston, shown above on horseback, had plans for freeing Texas from Mexican rule by force; he wanted to do it with the help of the Cherokee Indians. President Andrew Jackson, however, forbade him to attempt this revolution.

44

Stephen Austin   Jim Bowie   Davy Crockett

Stephen Austin, who had tried desperately to find a peaceful solution for the problems Texas had with Mexico, was forced to admit in 1835 that war was inevitable; he even served for a short time as military commander of the volunteer army. The frontiersman Jim Bowie served in the Texas army as a colonel and would meet his death in the Battle of the Alamo. Davy Crockett of Tennessee, a frontiersman and former congressman, would also fight and die at the Alamo.

ans responded by taking down rifles and muskets from wall pegs. Cannon on the plazas were manned.

Thirty thousand Texas colonists, with Comanche and other hostile Indian tribes on their flanks, were daring the might of a nation of seven million. They could count on no official aid from the United States, whose government refused to interfere in the affairs of Mexico. Sympathetic Southern states sent help secretly. A battalion of three hundred volunteers from Georgia reached Texas in December, 1835. Two companies from New Orleans arrived, and there were some other reinforcements, along with munitions and supplies.

Americans had taken on heavy odds before. Here were descendants of men who had fought Great Britain from 1775 to 1783, along with veterans and sons of veterans of the War of 1812. These Texans promptly showed they were tough and determined. When a detachment of one hundred Mexican cavalry were sent by Colonel Ugartechia, commander of the garrison at San Antonio, to the town of Gonzales, east of San Antonio, to demand the surrender of its brass cannon, a Texas leader trained the gun on the horsemen and raised a sign telling them to come and take it. The cavalrymen made a halfhearted attempt and then retreated. Texans chased them, hauling the cannon. They opened fire with it and charged. The Mexicans, with the loss of one man killed, were routed.

That little fight on October 2, 1835,

45

was called "the Lexington of the Texas Revolution." The brass 6-pounder had fired a shot heard round Mexico. The war was on.

More and more Texans answered the call to arms. A soldier of the War of 1812, Ben Milam, had recently escaped from a Mexican jail; he was fated soon to die in action. Edward Burleson, a renowned Indian fighter, possessed a flair for command. The frontiersman Erastus "Deaf" Smith was a crack shot, admired even among Texans who prided themselves on their marksmanship. One settler's knife drew more

Santa Anna, shown here in a daguerreotype of about 1850, had long been a political force in Mexico when the Texas revolt began. He had participated in the overthrow of the shaky empire of Agustín Iturbide in 1823.

attention than his rifle. It belonged to James Bowie. His weapon, scabbarded at his belt, had been invented by himself or his brother. Death was waiting for him as it was for Milam and others; but the Bowie knife and the manner of his dying would carry on his fame.

William Barret Travis was fiercely eager to fight for the rights of the colonists; so was another firebrand, James Walker Fannin. Stalwart Davy Crockett, a noted scout, had been a United States congressman. "Betsy," the long rifle he cradled, had rung out in the War of 1812 and in many an Indian fight.

A name that would lead all the rest was that of big Sam Houston, six feet two. He was also a veteran of the War of 1812 and an active Indian fighter, although the Cherokee, his lifelong friends, had adopted him into their tribe when he was fourteen. An able soldier, Sam Houston was also a statesman; like Crockett he had served in Congress. He took rank with Austin as a great leader under the Lone Star flag, now unfurled for battle.

The tread of booted feet and the pounding hoofs of horses drummed on the prairie. Bands of Texans closed in on the Mexican garrisons. They marched toward Goliad and San Antonio.

Ben Milam led a night attack on the small Mexican garrison at Goliad, due south of Gonzales, and on the San Antonio River. A sentry challenged and fired. He was killed almost as soon as the crimson flash of his musket flared in the darkness of that night of

General Martín Cos (above) was sent to Texas with troops in September, 1835, by General Santa Anna to increase the Mexican government's control over all of its citizens.

In 1837 General Anastasio Bustamante (above) managed to gain the presidency of Mexico, replacing Santa Anna. In 1841, however, Santa Anna would depose Bustamante.

October 9, 1835. Texan axes crashed through the door of the headquarters of the Mexican colonel in command. He and twenty-five soldiers quickly surrendered while the rest fled. Three hundred stands of arms, several pieces of artillery, and ten thousand dollars in money and stores were captured—a splendid prize. The Texans held Goliad. It had been easily won but would be bloodily lost.

In early October, Austin sent ninety-two men under Bowie and Fannin marching toward San Antonio, with a main body under himself following. The advance force camped on the plain outside the town. San Antonio was garrisoned by four hundred troops commanded by General Cos. On the morning of October 27, 1835, squadrons of Mexican lancers, accompanied by a cannon, burst through the mist and charged the Texan camp. A solid sheet of lead met them. The Texans worked in pairs, one man loading while the other fired, so there was never a gap in the volleys of musketry.

Three charges were shattered. One gun crew after another was shot down around the cannon. Whooping Texans overran it and turned it against the enemy. In half an hour, with only one man killed, they had carried the field. It was strewn with a hundred Mexican dead and wounded. The victors would have rushed on to storm San Antonio at once if Austin, arriving with the main force, had not halted them in order to reorganize. The siege of San Antonio was to last another six weeks.

This picture of the fall of the Mexican-held fort of San Antonio de Bexar in December, 1835, to the Texans was used as an illustration for an adventure story published in 1846. The Texans at left — guided by their standard bearer — are attacking the remaining Mexican defenders of the fort at right. The actual surrender of General Cos and his troops came in the Alamo—across the river from Bexar—to which they had retreated.

General Austin was sent to the United States to seek help for Texas, now in full revolt, by the general convention of Texas leaders who met at San Felipe on November 3. General Edward Burleson took over the dissatisfied, impatient army outside San Antonio. An officer stepped into his tent and emerged to assemble the Texans. He waved his hat and called out: "Who will follow old Ben Milam [into San Antonio]?"

Three hundred volunteers roared an answer. That night they slipped into the outskirts of town and were ready to launch an attack before dawn. A sentry yelled an alarm. Though "Deaf" Smith's ears might not have heard, there was nothing wrong with his shooting eye. A bullet from his rifle killed the guard.

If the Texans had thought Mexicans would not fight, they learned better now. For five days combat raged from street to street, from house to house. Ben Milam was killed leading an assault. On General Cos's order, a red flag was waved from the church tower. It signaled: no quarter, no mercy for the enemies of Mexico—any man left alive when we have conquered will be shot. Texans were to see that flag of ominous hue again.

But now it was about to be lowered for a white one. The last defenses were stormed. General Cos, his loss 150 in killed and wounded to the Texans' twenty-eight, surrendered on December 10, 1835. His disarmed army was allowed to march back to Mexico after

On March 2, 1836, a convention meeting at Washington-on-Brazos declared Texas an independent nation and appointed David G. Burnet (above) president of a temporary government. The convention met at the blacksmith's shop below, the first Texas capitol.

he had given his parole (word of honor) that he and his men would not fight again. That promise would last only until Santa Anna broke it for him.

The victory at San Antonio was to prove costly. While the siege had been going on, the army outside the city had swelled to more than a thousand men —Texas colonists, American volunteers (including the companies from New Orleans), and adventurers. One of these was Dr. James Grant, a Scotsman who had become a Mexican citizen, and who owned large tracts of land near Matamoros, a port at the mouth of the Rio Grande for the rich silver mining districts of Mexico. Grant suggested that an invading expedition be sent to Matamoros to detach from Mexico all the rich mining states north

of a line which had been drawn due west from Tampico.

The soldiers were bored; hundreds of Texan fighters were leaving San Antonio every day and drifting back to their homes. The American volunteers were also beginning to think the war was over.

Two hundred volunteers abandoned San Antonio in late December and started south under James Fannin to seize Matamoros, three hundred miles away. They gathered, with more volunteers, at Goliad.

Only 104 destitute men were left to face the cold winter under the command of Colonel J. C. Neill, who wrote the provisional council that the "Matamoros stampede" had carried off most of the food, clothing, medicine, and horses. The "Matamoros fever," as Sam Houston called it, had already split the provisional council at San Felipe. The split was not healed until the convention met in March. The groundwork for disaster was already laid for the Alamo.

The year 1835 waned into 1836. The handful of Texas soldiers manning San Antonio believed that the enemy, driven far to the south, was unlikely to return before spring brought green grass to feed their horses. Only Jim Bowie, who held joint command with Neill, was worried. He knew that a winter invasion, with dry mesquite grass for forage, was entirely possible.

On February 11, Neill released his command to William Travis, who had just marched to San Antonio with twenty-six men. At the same time, Davy Crockett arrived, in command of twelve Tennessee volunteers.

Named for *los alamos*, cottonwood trees lining the water ditches beside it, the Alamo, across the San Antonio River, had been abandoned as a mission in 1793. It had since been used as a fort, but with two fortified places in the city, there were no men to man it, although they did build ditches and redoubts.

The Alamo was not yet a name to be bitterly remembered.

A young Texan stood on watch in the tower of a San Antonio church on the morning of February 23, 1836. Suddenly, far across the plain, he caught sight of pennons, lances, helmets, and sabers gleaming in the sunlight. Mexican cavalry! He tugged frantically at the bell rope, and the clapper pealed a mad alarm. When Travis ran up the tower steps, the horsemen had vanished into the swales. But the lookout had not been dreaming. Scouts rode out and galloped back with confirmation. A force of 1,500 of the enemy was at hand, and it was only the advance guard. Santa Anna and 6,000 troops were not far behind. They had made a hard march

OVERLEAF: *This painting by the nineteenth-century Texas artist Robert Onderdonk shows Davy Crockett (center) in his last stand at the Alamo on March 6, 1836. He is using his famous rifle "Betsy" as a club to beat off the rapidly advancing Mexican troops who have succeeded in breaching the walls of the mission. It is believed that Crockett was one of the last defenders of the Alamo.*

This 1885 painting of the final Mexican assault on the Alamo is thought to be the most accurate view of the battle available. Mexican troops are shown approaching the fortifications from all sides; the defenders are seen firing from the mission at right.

from Laredo across wastelands with little water and no forage, a feat of superb endurance.

There was no time to lose. Travis ordered the town abandoned and the Alamo occupied. He and Jim Bowie, with the racking cough of developing pneumonia, led 150 men to the fort. Captain Almaron Dickinson, his wife Sue behind him on his horse, their baby in his arms, galloped through the gate. Couriers raced off with appeals for help. In answer thirty-two volunteers from Gonzales would slip through the Mexican lines to reinforce the garrison. That was all. The courier to Goliad, James Butler Bonham, rode back alone to the Alamo. Fannin could send no help. He, too, was being attacked. Though Bonham could bring no aid, he had returned to die with his comrades if need be.

Riflemen manned the walls, and gunners loaded the fourteen cannon. From a staff floated a flag of thirteen stripes of red and white on a blue background, in its center a lone star blazoned with the word Texas.

The Mexican army flooded into San Antonio and lapped out around the Alamo. Santa Anna sent a demand for unconditional surrender with the threat that every man would be "put to the sword in case of refusal." His

messenger was dismissed with a cannon shot to speed him. On February 23, the historic siege commenced.

Over in San Antonio another flag rose—that deadly, blood-red one that declared no quarter would be given. Massed bands played the attacking columns into action, and the tune they blared carried the same menace as the flag. It was "Deguello"—an old Moorish chant summoning men to the cutting of throats.

Davy Crockett's long rifle, "Betsy," picked off the first Mexican soldier. Others dropped under the unerring

fire from the walls, and the columns recoiled before the blasts of the Texans' cannon. No mere show of force would take the Alamo. It must be stormed. Santa Anna began to ring it with entrenchments, massing his infantry and moving up his own artillery. Around the encircling force he stationed an outer cordon of cavalry. Not only would the horsemen beat off any relief that might appear but they would prevent the retreat of his own storm troops if they wavered in the final assaults.

The days of the siege dragged by.

No Texan had been more than scratched, but Bowie was down, so sick he could not leave his cot. Powder and cannon balls were dwindling. And everyone knew now that no more help would come and that they must soon be overwhelmed by the Mexican might. Knowing he could expect no mercy from Santa Anna, Travis called for a fight to the death on March 3. With his sword he drew a line on the ground and asked all volunteers to step over it. Every man crossed. (Some say one refused and escaped from the Alamo.) Jim Bowie could not move, but he called to comrades to carry his cot over the line.

On March 6, the thirteenth day of the siege, Santa Anna received reinforcements. His batteries smashed open two breaches in the walls. In the cold pre-dawn, 2,500 assault troops with scaling ladders closed in on all four sides of the Alamo. Three sentries outside the walls were bayoneted before they could cry out. Then followed a bugle blast, bands blaring the soul-chilling strains of "Deguello," the roar of cannonading and musketry, and screams of "*Viva* Santa Anna." Travis shouted: "Come on, men! The Mexi-cans are on us! We'll give 'em hell!"

A sheet of flame ran around the walls, as long rifles cracked and the artillery thundered. One Mexican soldier who lived through that devastating fire remembered that forty men fell around him in a few moments. What was left of the assault waves ebbed back over a mass of bodies.

Jim Bowie, too weak to get up, lay on his cot in the almost pitch-dark Alamo chapel, attended by Mrs. Dickinson and several Mexican women. Two pistols, given him by Davy Crockett, and his knife rested ready to his hand. Grimly he listened to gun-fire break out again and soar to a crescendo.

Santa Anna could allow no respite after that first slaughter. He ordered

The Alamo (below) was a weed-choked ruin in 1848 when this water color was made; it bore little resemblance to the fort that withstood a fierce and bloody thirteen-day siege.

an all-out attack. Troops converged on the fort. Scaling ladders were flung against the walls. Texans shot and clubbed the top climbers and shoved the ladders back to crash to the ground with their burdens. But now the enemy was bursting through the breaches. Defending riflemen, targets for fire from front and rear, toppled from the parapets. Cannon could no longer be sufficiently depressed to fire into the masses below. Across the barrel of one of them slumped Travis, shot through the forehead. Bonham and Dickinson were also among those killed.

The end was near. Volleys and stabbing bayonets cut down the Texans. Davy Crockett, his right arm broken by a bullet, fired with his left till the stock of his rifle was shattered. At last he went down, his knife buried to the hilt in the chest of a Mexican soldier, with fifteen other corpses around him. Bowie was waiting when the enemy rushed into the dark chapel. Pistols flamed from his cot. For seconds the famous Bowie knife slashed right and left before sabers and bayonets thrust past it, and it fell from a dead hand.

Echoes of the last shot had faded when Santa Anna left San Antonio and crossed the river. He rode past the still forms of the many soldiers who had died to win the Alamo for him—as many as 1,600, one of his officers estimated. Five Texan prisoners were brought out before the victorious army on parade. A general asked mercy for them. In cold fury Santa Anna turned his back, and Mexican bayonets fin-

Susana Dickinson (above), wife of one of the Alamo defenders, stayed in the mission during the siege to nurse the wounded soldiers. She survived to report what had happened.

ished the survivors. Mrs. Dickinson, her child, the Mexican women, and two Negro slave boys were spared. But Santa Anna, true to his threat, had left no fighting man alive. Oil was poured over 182 heaped-up bodies, and they were burned.

Texas had a battle cry, bought with blood: "Remember the Alamo!"

Texas also had independence. One hundred and fifty miles to the northeast of San Antonio, while the Alamo was under bombardment, a convention of colonists at Washington-on-Brazos declared the independence of Texas on March 2, 1836, and appointed David Burnet provisional president.

When the United States annexed Texas, typically Mexican towns like San Antonio—seen above in an 1849 painting—remained unchanged. This busy square, lined with adobe buildings, is filled with burros and with carts.

Lone Star
Joins the Union

Santa Anna's generals led their troops onward to wipe the American settlements off the map of Texas. By March 14, the town of Refugio was taken. Stephen Austin could find no help in the United States except for a few volunteers. In those dark days the Texan cause seemed all but lost. General Sam Houston, in desperate haste, was organizing and drilling an army. Colonel Fannin still held Goliad with over four hundred men from the stalled Matamoros expedition.

Other members of the expedition had stopped at San Patricio, Texas, and Santa Anna had dispatched General José Urrea to destroy them. They were wiped out on March 2. Urrea moved

John C. Calhoun   Daniel Webster   Henry Clay

*These American statesmen were vitally concerned with the question of the
annexation of the slave-holding Republic of Texas. Calhoun, a firm believer
in slavery, was in favor; Webster, an ardent abolitionist, was opposed;
and Clay, hoping to keep it out of the 1844 election, tried to be neutral.*

on toward Goliad. Fannin was determined not to be caught in the fort and overwhelmed as the men at San Patricio and the defenders of the Alamo had been. With the enemy following, he marched out on March 19, 1836. In the open prairie he ordered a halt for rest. His officers urged him to go on. Only two and one-half miles farther was a creek which would assure an ample supply of water. Fannin, contemptuous of Mexicans as fighters, curtly refused to stir.

Seven hundred of General Urrea's Mexican dragoons swooped down at a gallop. Twelve hundred infantrymen surrounded the halted column. Distant dust on the prairie signaled the approach of still more—five hundred reinforcements with artillery, fresh from

triumph at the Battle of the Alamo.

The Texans formed their wagon train into a hollow square, cannon at each corner. All day riflemen and gunners beat back repeated onslaughts. Fannin, though early wounded in the thigh, carried on a stubborn defense, but water soon gave out, and now the Texans could not reach the creek. His men were tortured by thirst. There was no water to swab and cool the bores of the cannon, so hot from firing that new powder charges would have exploded during loading. The artillery ceased fire, and the rifles alone held off enemy charges till night darkened the field.

On the morning of March 20, 1836, Fannin surrendered on condition that his men would be treated as prisoners of war. They were herded back to Goliad where Urrea received orders from Santa Anna to ignore the surrender terms and shoot the prisoners.

A week later, on Palm Sunday, March 27, 1836, unwounded men, mostly volunteers who had come from the United States in January, were marched out of town believing they were being sent back to the United States. Suddenly their guards wheeled and leveled their muskets. An American cried out, "Boys, they are going to shoot us!" Volleys flashed. Three hundred and thirty-three soldiers, including three companies from Alabama, three from Georgia, and two from Kentucky, lay dead. Back in Goliad eighty-eight had been set aside to be spared, including surgeons to treat the Mexican wounded, but the Texans wounded from the fight on the prairie were slaughtered. Fannin was the last to die, facing his executioners with courage. Only twenty-seven men had managed to escape.

Many settlers abandoned their homes and hurried their families toward the safety of Louisiana. Their only remaining protection was Houston's little army of eight hundred men, and they too were retreating northeastward toward Louisiana. Santa Anna and his army pursued them, burning towns on the march.

General Sam Houston did not retreat for long. He doubled back and moved quietly forward toward a pleasant, tree-fringed plain where the San Jacinto River flows into a great arm of Galveston Bay. There the Mexicans were resting behind a barricade they had raised, never suspecting that the Texans had approached. Houston kept his men hidden in the woods and did not attack Santa Anna's 910 soldiers but let them be joined by 500 more. Meanwhile he sent "Deaf" Smith and a detail to burn a bridge that would cut off the Mexicans' retreat to the southwest. Marshes and bayous would block them in other directions.

The stage was set for the crucial Battle of San Jacinto. On that afternoon of April 21, 1836, Houston led his army out onto the plain—cavalry on the right, artillery in the center of the infantry line. "Trail arms. Forward!" the General shouted. Sam Houston rode ahead on his big white stallion, Saracen. Close behind were dragged the cannon, two of them called "the Twin Sisters." Swung around, they opened a furious fire, using broken horseshoes in their loads when their regular ammunition gave out.

The Mexicans, completely surprised, ran from camp to man the barricade. Crimson volleys blazed along its length. Not a single shot in reply was fired by the Texas infantry. They came on steadily. At forty yards they poured a deadly fusillade into the closely packed enemy ranks.

Above the roar of battle rose the war cries that here became famous: "Remember the Alamo!" "Remember Goliad!" The Texans fired again, point-blank now, full in the face of the enemy. They burst through the barri-

Once Texas got its freedom from Mexico it adopted the Lone Star flag (above) as the official flag of the Republic of Texas. It was at the Battle of San Jacinto (right) on April 21, 1836, that Texans, defeating the Mexican army of General Santa Anna, won that freedom. The battle flag below, carried by a company of Kentucky volunteers fighting in the Battle of San Jacinto, is thought to have been the only Texan banner flying during the fight.

cade, parrying bayonet thrusts with rifle barrels, jabbing with butts and stabbing with bowie knives, for they had no bayonets of their own.

Five bullets thudded into Saracen. As the white stallion dropped, Houston jumped clear. Somebody brought him another horse, but scarcely had the General mounted when he was painfully wounded in one ankle. He charged on with his men through the Mexican tents where his second horse was shot. Raging Texans slaughtered the enemy as relentlessly as their comrades had been cut down at the Alamo. Mexican pleas for mercy went unheeded. Here and there Texan officers knocked aside revengeful rifles and urged their men to take prisoners.

It was all over in twenty minutes.

Almost the whole Mexican army of fourteen hundred men had been killed or captured, with the Texans' loss only six killed and twenty-five wounded.

One of the few to escape was Santa Anna. When he saw the day was lost, he galloped off on a fast horse until he reached the marshes. There he abandoned his mount and stole away under cover of the tall grass, where he hid during the night. The next day three Texan riders spotted him. Santa Anna, who had managed to change from his glittering uniform into a plain one, declared he was only a cavalry trooper. One of his captors wanted to shoot him. The other men, more kindhearted, insisted on taking him back unharmed to camp. He was recognized when Mexican soldiers jumped up to

Vice President George Dallas (above) was honored on his inauguration in 1845 by the new state of Texas, which named a small town after him.

President James K. Polk

salute, exclaiming, *"El Presidente!"*

Santa Anna's life hung by a thread. Let him face a firing squad, Texans demanded—this butcher who had ordered no quarter at the Alamo and the massacre of the Goliad prisoners. Santa Anna protested that he had only been obeying a decree of the Mexican Congress. It was Houston who spared him in the belief he would be valuable as a hostage to prevent further attacks on Texas. Santa Anna signed a treaty with Houston recognizing the Republic of Texas. The *Presidente* was then sent, a hostage, with a Texan delegation to Washington, D.C., to negotiate with Andrew Jackson's administration and bring about annexation, or at least American recognition of Texas. After futile discussions Jackson had him put aboard an American warship and sent back to Mexico. The treaty Santa Anna had signed with Houston was repudiated by Mexico, and for a little while

Late in 1845 President Polk appointed John Slidell commissioner to Mexico. Slidell's instructions were to set the Texas border at the Rio Grande and to try to buy New Mexico and California. Herrera, president of Mexico when Slidell arrived, could not receive him because anti-American feeling in Mexico was too strong. When Herrera's government fell in December, 1845, his successor, Paredes, would not receive Slidell because he was himself violently anti-American.

he was in disgrace. But it was not long before he was back in power.

He helped defend Veracruz when French warships bombarded it in 1838 to punish Mexico for damages to French property sustained in Mexico's revolution. Santa Anna's loss of a leg in the fight made him a hero. He managed to make himself a general again, then, in 1841, was re-elected president of Mexico. Only ten years after the Battle of San Jacinto, Americans would

John Slidell

Mariano Paredes

José Herrera

have to reckon with him once more.

San Jacinto was a decisive victory. It changed the whole spirit of Texas from near-despair to bright hope. Remaining Mexican armies marched away with trailing banners. On the first Monday in September, 1836, the first elections were held in the new Republic of Texas. Sam Houston was elected president for the first of two terms. Stephen Austin—one of Houston's opponents—only polled 587 votes to the war hero's 5,119. Houston at once appointed Austin to serve as secretary of state.

In Washington, President Jackson was testing the opinion of the Senate and the public on annexation of Texas. Strong forces in the Whig party, led by Henry Clay, were against such a dangerous move at that time, espe-

cially in view of criticism from abroad that annexation would amount to an out-and-out land-grab. Mexico, refusing to recognize either Santa Anna's peace treaty or the new republic, threatened war with the United States if Texas was annexed as a state of the Union. In the face of a coming election, Jackson hedged on the question until Martin Van Buren, his Democratic political heir, had been safely elected. Once the election was won, Jackson was willing to recognize the Republic of Texas on March 3, 1837, but he did not press for annexation.

Most of the people of the new republic were eager for its annexation to the United States. At any time from that year on the United States had only to stretch out its hand to add a big state to the Union.

Fear of war with Mexico was not the only factor that delayed Texas' entry. There were five thousand slaves in Texas. In 1820 the Missouri Compromise, by adding one slave state (Missouri) and one free state (Maine) to the Union, had kept the all-important balance of free and slave states in the Senate, where the two groups were exactly divided.

In 1837, Elijah Lovejoy, a prominent abolitionist (or antislavery agitator) was murdered by a mob in Illinois. At once the abolitionists set upon the whole proslavery faction, and the cause for Texas' annexation suffered.

A rumor was started that a plan was afoot to annex Texas not as one state but as "five or six more slaveholding

65

states to this Union." The furor was so great that no politician dared take a stand on Texas again until 1844.

Meanwhile, more settlers poured into Texas, until in 1836 the population exceeded thirty thousand. Both England and France were maneuvering for treaties with the new republic. Even in the face of international interference there were many Americans who believed it would be wrong to go to war with Mexico over Texas. Furthermore, although the United States was far wealthier and more highly populated, there were more trained soldiers in the Mexican army than in the American. Mexican cavalry was rated better than that of the United States by European observers, and cavalry would be important in the

In the 1900 painting above, Sam Houston (center), lying wounded, accepts the surrender of defeated Mexican commander Santa Anna — standing at left in white breeches — after the Battle of San Jacinto. The man seated on the stump at right, cupping his ear to hear the surrender terms, is "Deaf" Smith.

theater of warfare across the border.

But the tide of opinion slowly began to turn toward war when United States relations with Mexico were disturbed by a series of incidents of mistreatment of Americans in Mexican territory. United States ships, visiting Mexican ports on legitimate errands, were delayed and their officers insulted. In April, 1840, numbers of Americans and other foreigners living in California were suddenly arrested, beaten, and thrown into prison. Then they were—as Mexican authorities admitted—expelled from the province illegally. American and Texan traders were sent by Texas' president, Mirabeau Lamar, to Santa Fe where they were seized by the Mexican government in June, 1841. They were ordered on a barbaric forced march through the New Mexican desert, where many of them died. The survivors spent months in Santa Anna's prisons in Mexico City. Such harsh and brutal treatment roused intense feeling against Mexico.

Then there were long-standing claims for damages against Mexico by American citizens for property losses suffered in Mexico's revolution. It was agreed by both nations that the matter be settled by an international commission, headed by the King of Prussia, which began investigations in 1841. (In 1843 an award to the United States of two million dollars was made. Mexico paid three installments out of twenty and let the rest lapse.)

In December, 1841, Houston was elected president of Texas for his second term. News that he was negotiating a treaty with England alarmed Washington, for England was trying to persuade Mexico to recognize the Republic of Texas, if Texas would promise never to join the Union. Annexation pressure was revived in Congress, as Houston no doubt intended that it should be. But Santa Anna, again president of Mexico, noti-fied the United States in 1843 that Mexico would consider annexation "equivalent to a declaration of war."

By 1844 the old dispute over the conflicting claims of England and the United States to the Oregon territory had flared up again. The temper of the United States was changing; there was talk of war over the Oregon boundary: "Fifty-four forty or fight!" would soon be a Democratic slogan. Fear that the old enemy, England, was pressing from the north in Oregon and from the south in Texas, caused a new demand for expansion to sweep the country. In June President Tyler made a strong attempt to annex Texas, but a hostile Senate—unsure of public opinion—refused him.

A new presidential election was at hand. Henry Clay, the Whig candidate, and Martin Van Buren, who expected to be the Democratic candidate, also failed to read national opinion when they made a public pact to keep the Texas question out of the election. Ex-President Jackson, in retirement at his Tennessee home, The Hermitage, was more astute. He called for another of his Democratic protégés, James K. Polk, and told him that he could win the Democratic nomination, and the election, if he promised the country "All of Oregon, all of Texas"—for such a promise would please both the North and the South. Polk took Jackson's advice and won the election of 1844. After nine years, Houston and Texas had helped make a President!

By joint resolution on March 1, 1845,

Congress invited Texas to become a state of the Union—Tyler's last act as President. On March 4, James K. Polk took office. Three weeks after his inauguration Mexico broke off relations with the United States.

Preparations for war on a grand scale commenced in Mexico. President Polk, with the Oregon dispute still unsettled, and with war with England a dangerous possibility, countered by ordering General Zachary Taylor with fourteen hundred troops to Corpus Christi on the Texas coast, where he arrived on July 31, 1845. Eight months later, in March, 1846, Taylor sent troops from Corpus Christi south to the mouth of the Rio Grande.

An attempt at a peaceful settlement was made by Polk in November, 1845, when he sent John Slidell to Mexico City to try to buy California and New Mexico for thirty million dollars. His mission failed.

By December the slogan from an expansionist magazine that it was America's "Manifest Destiny to overspread the continent," was being heard all over the country.

On May 13, 1846, the United States declared war on Mexico.

These soldiers of the Republic of Texas, herded into a Mexican fort at Salado in February, 1843, were captured while fighting a Mexican border attack. Seventeen of the 176 Texans were killed brutally by the Mexicans.

"Old Rough and Ready"

It was a little army numbering about 3,500 men that Zachary Taylor met on the Rio Grande. Even when later reinforced, it would face three or four times as many Mexicans. Indeed the whole United States Army then numbered only 7,200 men. It would have to be filled out with volunteers and state troops such as the Texas Rangers and the Louisiana militia which accompanied Taylor.

Taylor's force was to be the first thrust of a four-pronged attack on Mexico. From Fort Texas (later called Fort Brown) on the Rio Grande he would cross the river to take the Mexican Gulf coast town of Matamoros. From there he was to march inland to Monterrey. Another field army was to be assembled at San Antonio under the command of General John Ellis Wool, and would invade the province of Chihuahua, due south of El Paso, Texas. A third army, commanded by Stephen Watts Kearny, was to drive southwest from Fort Leavenworth, Kansas, and take Santa Fe, New Mexico. Thence it would march westward and, with the United States Navy closing in from the sea, capture California. The fourth attack was to come later, by way of a force under the command of General Winfield Scott. Scott would sail, in November, 1846, with his army from New Orleans, stop at Matamoros, and then sail south, taking Tampico and Veracruz. Then Scott would march on Mexico City.

Weapons for the most part were out-of-date. With the exception of some of the regulars, there was a lack of training and discipline, and too many soldiers would die in battle before they learned those essentials.

When General Taylor, veteran of many an Indian fight, marched to the border river, soldiers remembered his tough campaigns against the Seminole in the Florida swamps. It was the Florida campaigns that had won him his nickname—and rhymes like this one which were made up about him:

> "I knew him first," the soldier said,
>   Among the Everglades,
> When we gave the savage redskins
>   Our bayonets and our blades.
> I think I hear his cheerful voice,
>   "On, column! Steady! Steady!"
> So handy and so prompt was he,
>   We called him Rough and Ready.

Few of Taylor's men cared that no general ever dressed less like one than Taylor. In startling contrast to the gorgeously uniformed Santa Anna, Old Zach wore a broad-brimmed straw hat

General Zachary Taylor — nicknamed Old Rough and Ready — posed for this portrait around 1846. A famous Indian fighter, Taylor was to win more fame as a general. His horse Old Whitey is shown behind him.

or an oilcloth cap, a blue-checked gingham coat or a duster, and odd pantaloons. Old Whitey, about to become his mount, was certainly no prancing charger, and his rider lounged in the saddle. Few were disturbed that Taylor never had commanded as many troops before. He was brave and confident, the sort of a general soldiers willingly follow.

Sun bronzed the marching infantry. Dust swirled high from under the hoofs of the horses of the dragoons and those of the artillery teams. Ahead of the 18-pounder siege cannon, drawn by oxen, rolled the light field guns of four flying batteries, so called because of their swiftness in galloping into action. On March 28, 1846, Taylor's men made camp at Fort Brown and Point Isabel, located at Brazos Island at the mouth of the Rio Grande.

Across the river around the town of Matamoros lay the Mexican army. Like the American force, it too lacked training and discipline. Its infantry was armed with discarded British muskets. Its artillery usually was poorly served and would continue to be until foreigners, including American deserters, were recruited to man it. The cavalry, mostly lancers, were fine horsemen, but their mounts were too light to meet the heavier horses of United States dragoons in the shock of a charge. Yet these horses were nimble and fast, and the cavalrymen who rode them boasted they could break an enemy square with their lances or by throwing their lassos and dragging

men from its ranks. There were too many generals and too many officers in the army who paid little or no attention to the welfare of their troops. But the Mexican soldier could make long marches, and he was often a hard fighter, as Texans could testify.

The two armies eyed each other across the river. Their bands struck up. The Americans played "Hail Columbia," "Yankee Doodle," and "The Star-Spangled Banner," while the Mexicans answered with the tuneful melodies of their own country. Sometimes a rooster, the mascot of a United States regiment, crowed lustily.

Hostilities were not far off. An American colonel rode off on a scout and never came back. A detail, sent to search for him, was attacked, and several men were killed. Mexico felt its territory had been invaded once Taylor had entered the debatable land, claimed by Texas and Mexico, which lay between the Nueces and Rio Grande rivers (see map on pages 110-111). Now a Mexican army under General Mariano Arista crossed the Rio Grande, captured a detachment of American dragoons on April 25, and marched around General Taylor's force to cut him off from his base of supplies. War had begun in deadly earnest.

Old Rough and Ready pulled back

These tents, pitched near the Gulf of Mexico, outside Corpus Christi, Texas, housed General Taylor's army. This view was drawn in October, 1845. On March 8, 1846, Taylor began to move his men to the Rio Grande.

to meet the threat in his rear. On May 8, the two armies—the Mexicans 6,000 strong, the Americans 2,300—drew near at Palo Alto, the place of the tall timber. General Taylor halted at a pond and ordered canteens filled. Thirst was not to torture his men this day as it had Fannin's Texans. His two 18-pounders lumbered into position behind their teams of ten yokes of oxen for each gun. The flying batteries dashed out and unlimbered beside them, well ahead of the infantry.

Battle lines formed, two American officers daringly rode across the whole front of the Mexican array, scouting and counting. Then the artillery of both armies opened with a roar. American shells burst among the enemy, but the Mexican gunners, with only round shot to fire and poor powder, could do little damage. Their cannon balls rolled through the tall grass, and American ranks opened to let them pass harmlessly. An artillery captain's dog chased them, barking furiously.

Cavalry, dragoons against lancers, clashed, as the Mexican flanks folded around the shorter American line to seize Taylor's wagon train. Rattling volleys from the Fifth and Third U.S. Infantry met them, and a hedge of bristling bayonets fended them off. It seemed the flying batteries were everywhere. Major Samuel Ringgold's guns shattered a Mexican column advancing to the attack.

The gun smoke shrouding the battlefield grew denser. Burning powder wads of the American artillery had set

American Captain Charles May—shown be-low on a brown mount—became a hero on May 9, 1846, in the Battle of Resaca de la Palma. Singlehanded, he took a Mexican battery and the commanding general (right).

the dry grass afire. Under the smoke screen, Captain James Duncan moved his guns to the flank and fired at the whole length of the Mexican line.

Bursting shells caused heavy Mexican casualties and sent the survivors fleeing in utmost confusion. A charge now might have decisively won the day, but Taylor dared not risk his smaller force in an all-out onslaught.

Once more the Mexican infantry bravely drove forward, their bands playing them on. Again a storm of artillery fire smashed into the on-coming ranks. A salvo of shrapnel, that deadly shell that explodes overhead

The picture at left shows the Battle of Palo Alto, fought on May 8, 1846. Some of Arista's troops are shown at the right; the officer on the white horse, riding with the American cavalry at left, is probably General Taylor on Old Whitey.

General Mariano Arista (right) commanded the Mexican army that Taylor's American army defeated in the Battle of Palo Alto. This portrait of Arista was painted in 1851, the year in which he became president of Mexico. He is wearing the elaborate uniform of a division general; his added rank of president is indicated by the band worn across his chest. Arista had been active in Mexico's fight for independence from Spain and also served in the Mexican army that tried to put down the revolt of the Texans in 1836.

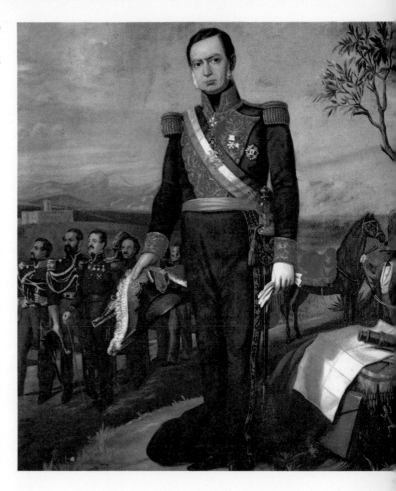

and sprays a cone of hurtling balls downward, riddled one of the bands. Its battle march was suddenly silenced. The attack faltered and recoiled before the iron hail. When a full moon rose over the smoldering prairie, the Mexican army had quit the field.

Palo Alto, the first pitched battle of the war, was an American victory that cost the Mexicans 320 killed and more than 400 wounded. United States losses were only 9 killed and 44 wounded, and 2 missing, but among the dead was that fine artilleryman Major Ringgold, who was severely wounded in battle and died shortly after being carried from the field. Next morning, May 9, General Taylor, following the retreating Mexicans, marched back toward the Rio Grande.

It was a land of wild beauty—rolling prairies and towering mountains—in which the Americans found themselves. Texas was still as Mexican in flavor as Old Mexico, soon to be invaded. Soldiers liked the towns and their pleasant plazas, the gay fandangos, and especially the pretty *señoritas.* Men in blue watched Mexican *caballeros,* singing and playing guitars, serenade *señoritas* on their balconies and decided to try it themselves. They strummed and sang a popular ditty with words written by the Scottish poet Robert Burns:

Green grow the Rushes, O!
Red are the Roses, O!
Kiss her quick and let her go
Before you get the mitten, O!

Of course, Mexican men were angry when their girls were courted by rivals. Jealously they made the first two words of the chorus into a term of hatred: Gringo. They vowed they would knife these interlopers, these Gringos, or kill them in battle. The Americans came back with an epithet of their own. Just let the Greasers try it, they said. So the two armies had names to call each other.

Near the Rio Grande the Mexicans

The gallant Major Samuel Ringgold (below), who died from wounds received in the Battle of Palo Alto, was one of the very first popular American heroes of the Mexican War.

were waiting for Taylor in a muddy ravine, hidden behind thorny thickets of chaparral. From their strong position their artillery opened heavy fire. Taylor occupied another ravine, called the Resaca de la Palma, and Lieutenant Randolph Ridgely, now commanding Ringgold's battery, galloped his six pieces forward to silence the enemy cannon. Lancers charged him when only one of his guns was unlimbered. A sergeant rammed in a round of canister on top of a shell and jerked the lanyard. Canister was short-range ammunition, a load of dozens of small iron balls in a tin can. It turned a cannon into a big shotgun. As it spat from the muzzle, all the lancers but four were cut down. Ridgely, single-handed, routed the survivors. When one of his lead drivers was shot from the saddle, the Lieutenant swung from his own mount onto the riderless horse and drove the team on. But the fire of the American artillery still could not clear the way.

Taylor trotted up on Old Whitey to see what was blocking his advance. Shell fragments whizzed close, some of them ripping through his coat. Neither rider nor horse flinched. That moment would be recorded in one of the songs that would help make Taylor President of the United States after the war:

In the thickest of the fight Old
    Zachary appeared.
The shot flew about him thick as
    any hail.
And the only injury he there received
Was a compound fracture of his
    brown coat tail.

The sketch above locates the Mexican and American positions at the beginning of the Battle of Resaca de la Palma. It is likely that this sketch was made on the battlefield. The American forces, ready to advance, are indicated at bottom. The headquarters of General Arista's Mexican army is seen at right of the road to Matamoros (top). The bodies of water on either side of the road are ponds.

The General's staff begged him to take cover with his target of a white horse. All he answered was, "Let us ride a little nearer. The balls will fall behind us." Then he ordered Captain May of the dragoons to charge the Mexican guns.

May, a tall man with a long black beard and flowing hair, spurred his black charger and led his squadron, every trooper stripped to the waist, at a headlong gallop. Sabers flashed as they swooped down on the batteries and drove the gunners from their posts. But they overrode the position, and before they could turn their horses the artillerymen had remanned their cannon and were blazing away again, and musket bullets were emptying dragoon saddles.

Taylor turned to the colonel of the Eighth Infantry. "Take those guns and keep them!" he snapped. The foot troops stormed forward and captured the guns of the Mexicans after a fierce struggle.

But the Mexicans, fighting valiantly and stubbornly, launched one more assault with their lancers. With its repulse they were finished. They broke and fled in panic, pursued by yelling infantrymen and scourged by the shells of the flying batteries. The fleeing mob ran for the river, where many were drowned in crossing. Americans seized the Mexican camp with fine booty of arms, ammunition, mules, wagons, colors, drums, and a banquet that had been prepared in anticipation of victory.

"Mexico or Death!"

Only now did the United States declare war against Mexico—a war which had already begun. A mail dispatch from General Taylor, stating that a Mexican army had invaded Texas and killed American dragoons, finally reached Washington. President Polk asked for the declaration, and Congress passed it. It was signed by Polk on May 13, 1846. Ten million dollars

were voted for war expenses, and the President was authorized to issue a call for fifty thousand volunteers.

War fever, heightened by news of the victories of Palo Alto and Resaca de la Palma, gripped the country except in New England, where they had not forgiven the admission of Texas as a slave state. More volunteers flocked to the colors than could be taken; they

Grande, and the lucky ones were sent upstream by steamboat. A march to the front was the lot of most of the troops, often through stifling dust or through ankle-deep mud.

The American volunteers were green recruits, and they did not know how to take care of themselves in the field. They drank unhealthy water and fell sick from it and from the rations of beans, pickled pork, and wormy hardtack. There was quarreling, stealing from Mexican residents, and drunkenness. Thousands of short-enlistment men who refused to sign up again sailed home. Taylor's army, which had increased to 15,000, dwindled by more than half in spite of the efforts of commanders and surgeons. Those who remained were tough soldiers able to cope with hardship.

So at the end of the summer of 1846, it was with 3,000 seasoned regular and as many fit volunteers that General Taylor marched 170 miles into Mexico. He was bound to besiege the walled citadel and city of Monterrey. For that task he had only a few siege guns; the light shells of the flying batteries could not breach those walls. And Monterrey was defended by 9,000 Mexicans with thirty-eight cannon. Among the crews manning the cannon there were some expert gunners—deserters from the American army.

Those gunners were the San Patricio

had to draw lots, and only the winners were accepted. People paraded through the streets carrying placards reading "Mexico or Death!"

Reinforcements for Taylor's army were assembled at New Orleans and shipped across the Gulf of Mexico. They landed near Point Isabel, Brazos Island. From there they marched to Boca del Rio at the mouth of the Rio

Battalion. It had been organized by Sergeant John Riley who, smarting from a reprimand, had deserted from one of Taylor's American regiments and had gone over to the enemy.

A stream of other deserters joined him. Some were Irishmen like Riley and red-headed. That gave the San Patricios another name: the *Colorados*, or Red Company. Others were foreign-born, too—recent immigrants to the United States from European countries other than Ireland. There were also some men in the company who were native Americans. Mexico promised them money and grants of land and appealed to the Roman Catholics among them to make common cause with a country of the same religion. American pay was low, and in some units discipline was so harsh that soldiers were flogged. Such were the reasons the San Patricios had for joining the Mexicans.

Riley trained them as artillery, because the Mexican army was weakest in good artillery men. The San Patricios were ready to fight to the death, for they knew that if they were captured, they would be executed as deserters and traitors.

General Taylor closed in on the old city of Monterrey, girdled by earthworks and strongholds, the Black Fort, and the Bishop's Palace. He sent General William J. Worth to cut the enemy's supply route. On September 20, 1846, the battle commenced as Taylor's light artillery opened fire. Its shells had no more effect against the massive walls of Monterrey's fortresses than stones from a slingshot.

Rain in torrents poured down on Worth's 2,000 advancing from the west. It could not quench their fighting spirit—nor could hunger when rations ran out. A column of Mexicans sallied out to meet them, and Mexican lancers charged the Texas cavalry. Outnumbered, the American horsemen were smashed back. On came the Mexican lancers again. Then two of the American flying batteries opened fire on the Mexicans and drove them back. With the Mexican horse and foot in retreat, Worth launched an attack on the fortifications.

Two high, steep hills and flanking forts barred the way. General Worth ordered his men to take the first hill.

Worth's troops first forded a cold, swift stream, holding their rifles clear of the water. Both hilltops and the ramparts of the forts blazed with smoke and flame. Bullets and cannon balls plunged down on the assault. But the Americans, struggling upward, were soon so close that the muzzles of the cannon could no longer be depressed enough to fire on them. Storming the cannon emplacements they seized guns and turned them on the enemy. By nightfall they were part way up the second hill.

At three o'clock in the blackness of the early morning, sergeants shook awake the weary soldiers. They were going to advance immediately. The sky turned gray as they climbed toward the unsuspecting Mexicans. There was

The American troops in the Chamberlain drawing above are storming the Bishop's Palace in Monterrey, Mexico, on September 22, 1846. The thick-walled palace was used as a fort by the Mexicans. The American attack on Monterrey began on September 20; Mexican troops surrendered four days later.

The United States army marching on Monterrey camped in this peaceful spot (below), three miles outside the city, on September 19, 1846. Their camp site, called Bosque de Santiago by the Mexicans, was renamed Walnut Springs by the homesick soldiers. This sketch was also made by Chamberlain.

General William J. Worth   *General John A. Quitman*   *General John E. Wool*

General Worth and General Quitman attacked Monterrey from opposite sides to soften the tough Mexican defenses. While the last defeated Mexican soldiers were leaving Monterrey on September 25, 1846, Wool began his 800-mile march to Mexico City.

The picture below of the defense of Monterrey by Mexican soldiers and civilians is one of a rare series of six contemporary prints of Mexican War battle scenes published in France. The Mexicans are beating back American troops trying to cross a barricade.

a rush, a yell, a sudden volley. The second hill shared the fate of the first.

The fortified Bishop's Palace still confronted them. A Mexican counter-attack might threaten the captured hills at any moment. Worth had no siege artillery to breach the palace's walls. The troops he ordered to the assault made the best of the situation by taking a 12-pound howitzer apart, dragging the sections up within range by ropes and straps and putting them together again. Soon the howitzer was flinging shrapnel over the walls that exploded in the interior of the palace.

Out from the gate burst Mexican soldiers. American howitzer and rifle volleys drove them back into the fortress. Once more the Americans rolled their 12-pound howitzer forward. It shattered the gate, and they broke into the palace. Despite the surge of blue-uniformed American soldiers, the Mexican defenders of the palace stood fast, however, and valiantly held their ground. Now the Americans heard a sudden shout from artillerymen behind them. "Throw yourselves flat!" They hit the ground. Over their heads the American howitzer belched a double charge of canister that finally crushed Mexican resistance. The palace and the western approach to the city of Monterrey were won.

Meanwhile the rest of the American army, attacking from the other side, was also meeting hard resistance. General Taylor pointed toward the northeastern corner of the city and said to his officers: "If you think you can take any of them little forts down there with the bay'net, you better do it."

They tried—infantry regulars, Maryland, Ohio, and Mississippi volunteers—but it was bloody work. Mexican fire from the forts and roofs and barred windows of the town strewed the ground with American dead. With dawn the attack was renewed.

The names of a dozen or more of the young officers in those fierce assaults would appear some twenty years afterwards on the roll of generals in the Civil War. They would include one commander in chief as president of the Confederacy, Jefferson Davis, now colonel of the Mississippi Rifles; U. S. Grant, who would lead the Union armies to final victory; George Gordon Meade, destined to win the Battle of Gettysburg; and Albert Sidney Johnston, the gallant Confederate commander killed at Shiloh.

Old Rough and Ready flung his troops at the enemy as if he were again fighting Indians in the Florida swamps. Well-armed and more numerous Mexicans behind fortifications were another matter. American casualties mounted. Combat through the city was particularly desperate, raging from house to house. Barricades across the narrow streets had to be blasted apart by cannon, but under the fire from above and in front artillerymen would not have lived to man their guns if they had not used a clever scheme. Tying ropes to the trail of a cannon, they loaded it in an alley or around a corner. Then they ran it rapidly out onto the street, fired a round, pulled the piece back behind cover by the ropes, and repeated the process. Infantrymen pickaxed holes in house walls, lit the fuse of a shell, jammed it in and blew a breach.

Bragg's battery ran out of ammunition. Lieutenant Ulysses S. Grant volunteered to have more shells sent. To reach the supply train he had to ride across the front of a long line of Mexican infantry. As he spurred past at top speed, a hundred muskets were leveled at him. The moment they flamed Grant swung down Indian-fashion behind the far side of his horse. Bullets whizzed over the empty saddle, and Grant dashed on unharmed to complete his mission.

In the end, sheer Yankee gallantry won the day—at a cost of 120 dead and 368 wounded. Worth, who had borrowed Taylor's 10-inch mortar, lobbed shells into the city's plaza. A Mexican bugle sounded the parley, and surrender was offered. Taylor agreed to terms which allowed the Mexican army to march away with all its small arms and six of its cannon. As the column left Monterrey, the Americans paid a silent tribute to an enemy who had fought well and hard. Only when the San Patricios— Riley and the other deserters — passed did their countrymen break into jeers and hisses.

This Chamberlain drawing shows the Americans attacking one of the Mexican strongholds at Monterrey. The man at far right in buckskins, holding a rifle, is a Texas Ranger.

Stephen Watts Kearny

Westward
to
California

Sonoma, California—seen above in 1847, after it had been claimed as an American town—was founded in 1835 by the Mexicans to prevent Russian fur traders from gaining control of northern California. It was at Sonoma in 1846 that an independent California republic was formed.

Much had happened in that year of 1846 before Taylor captured Monterrey, Mexico, in September.

Armed forces of the United States converged on California by sea and land. To add that Mexican province to the Union, along with New Mexico, was as important an objective of the war as defending the new state of Texas. President Polk and Congress were eager to gain territory by which the nation would span the continent all the way to the Pacific Ocean.

In June, just after the war had begun, a new banner had been unfurled in the Far West—the Bear Flag, on its folds a grizzly bear facing a red star. It was raised in revolt by American settlers of the Sacramento Valley in northern California. They were sparked by John Charles Frémont, explorer and soldier, who had come to California with an expedition of sixty men, and with secret orders from President Polk to help the small United States naval force in California waters

in the event of an all-out war with Mexico. Though the settlers, claiming they had won independence from Mexico, established the Republic of California, their struggle was no more than an entering wedge.

The American drive for the coveted province commenced when Colonel Stephen W. Kearny, a veteran of the War of 1812, was ordered to march his Army of the West from Fort Leavenworth, Kansas, and seize Santa Fe,

New Mexico. Thence he would be sent on to California. Meanwhile, the small Pacific squadron of the United States Navy under Commodore John D. Sloat was cruising off California. Sloat had been ordered by Secretary of the Navy George Bancroft to guard American interests in California. If the revolt in the province made any real headway, Sloat was to support it.

News that war with Mexico had begun did not reach the Commodore

until July, 1846. Then he landed blue-jackets and marines and captured the port of Monterey in western California. Sloat, old and ill, turned over his command to Robert F. Stockton. The naval force ashore now made preparations to march southward as Colonel Kearny advanced from the east.

A mighty march lay ahead of Kearny and his 1,660 men. They started for Santa Fe over the famous old trail of the traders. Kearny had a regiment

Kearny's Army of the West is shown at right as it passes the town of San Felipe, New Mexico, in the fall of 1846. Kearny left Fort Leavenworth, Kansas, in June, 1846, took Santa Fe in August, and completed the tortuous thousand-mile march from Santa Fe to San Diego, California, by December, 1846.

89

of Missouri riflemen under Colonel Alexander W. Doniphan, other infantry, dragoons, one battery of artillery, Indian scouts, and an ox-drawn wagon train. It was one of the greatest marches in our history they undertook, with nearly nine hundred miles stretching ahead. Through intense heat and waterless days, the column forced the pace. Many horses died, and most of the cavalry was compelled to shift saddles to mules.

Bent's Fort on the Arkansas River, Raton Pass, and the New Mexican village of Las Vegas at last lay behind them. Now they were nearing their goal. Thousands of Mexicans, it was said, held Santa Fe. Kearny was planning to swing off through the mountains for a flank attack when word came that the town's garrison had melted away. He pushed forward and on August 18, 1846, took it without firing a shot.

On September 25, Kearny marched for California with three hundred dragoons. On the way, he met the celebrated scout Kit Carson, who was carrying dispatches to Washington reporting that Sloat had landed and captured Monterey. Kearny sent the news on by another messenger and took Carson as his guide. Then he sent back the larger portion of his troops and entered California with one hundred men. There 150 Mexican lancers attacked Kearny's men, worn by privations, at San Pasqual in December.

Like a charge of medieval knights, the splendid horsemen galloped for-

ward in line, long wooden spears leveled. Thrusting and impaling, the lances broke the American ranks. At length, in a desperate rally, sabers, carbines, and cannon beat off the onslaught. Tough Stephen Kearny, twice wounded, drove on through to join up with Commodore Stockton's men in San Diego on December 12. Their combined forces numbered 559 men.

On January 8, 1847, an army under the Mexican governor waited in ambush beyond the San Gabriel River, which although shallow was a trap of treacherous quicksand. It clutched the hoofs of American artillery teams and the wheels of carriages as they tried to cross. Unless the cannon reached the opposite bank to cover a charge with their fire, the advance would be blocked.

The Commodore himself rode into the water. Defying the quicksand, he swung from the saddle and sternly grasped a rope on one of the pieces. "The guns shall pass over!" he roared. Willing hands tugged away with him, and the teams pulled their utmost. Mexican lancers came splashing in to overwhelm them in midstream, but volleys from marines and sailors beat them off, and the cannon crossed.

Kearny stepped forward, a pistol in each hand. "Now, Commodore," he announced to Stockton, "I am ready to charge." With the guns booming, army and navy blue surged over the Mexican horse and foot. At a loss of only three killed and seven wounded, American arms won the Battle of San

Gabriel, and with it all of California.

Colonel Doniphan, with nine hundred men, had been left at Santa Fe with orders to complete the conquest of New Mexico. He struck south in December, defeated the enemy at El Brazito, and took the town of El Paso on December 26, 1846. There his artillery joined him after a heroic march in which it faced near-starvation and both a snowstorm and a sandstorm. A special welcome was in order, the El Paso garrison decided. Hastily a captured Mexican cannon was loaded with a blank charge, but no wad could be found to tamp the powder. An infantryman kicked off his boots, stripped off his socks and offered them as

The American colonists at Sonoma, California, raised a Bear Flag that resembled the flag above when they declared independence from Mexico in June, 1846. This revolt broke the Mexican hold on northern California.

The picture below shows a group of United States marines raising the American flag at Monterey, California, on July 7, 1846; Commodore John D. Sloat's Pacific squadron, seen in the background, is firing a salute.

wadding. When the cannon banged, another soldier let out a wild yell as he was hit in the face. Though he was not hurt, he yelled even louder when he found out what the wad was and demanded the gun crew be punished.

Doniphan invaded the province of Chihuahua and fought the Battle of Sacramento on February 26, 1847.

Against a hill fort, manned by a superior force of Mexicans, the tall Missouri colonel mounted an attack on wheels. His cavalry preceded his big wagon train, which advanced in four parallel columns of one hundred wagons each. Hidden between them were infantry and artillery. Flags flew from the prairie schooners plunging and careening across a gulch toward the fort. Out from that canvas screen burst the guns. At a range of half a mile, shells burst among the Mexicans. The American guns limbered, charged, and opened again at fifty yards. Infantry rushed in and took the fort against fierce resistance in hand-to-hand combat. The field was won at a cost of one killed and eight wounded to some 600 Mexican casualties.

When Doniphan and his sturdy men finally marched back to Missouri to be mustered out, they had covered 3,600 miles.

Now that victory in the West was won, the decisive battles must be fought in Mexico itself. Who would be

An American sailor serving under Stockton in the naval sea and land assault on southern California made these sketches (above and below) in 1847. American victory on the plains of La Mesa (above) on January 9, 1847, gave the United States control of Los Angeles for the second time; it had been won and lost in 1846. Mexican lancers like the one below fought valiantly at La Mesa.

the spearhead of the drive for the capital? Was General Taylor's army to thrust south through the mountains? Or would the main attack be made by another force which would sail through the Gulf of Mexico, land at Veracruz, and then fight its way westward to Mexico City?

President Polk's administration had to make the choice, and the question was not only a military but a political one. Polk was a Democrat. The two leading generals, Scott and Taylor, belonged to the opposing party, the Whigs (many of whose members later became Republicans). Both generals wanted to be the next President of the United States. Polk, as leader of the Democratic party, was determined to see to it that neither general gained too much political advantage from the war. Zachary Taylor, who had already become a national hero because of his victories at Palo Alto, Resaca de la Palma, and Monterrey, was gaining

political strength rapidly. Although General Winfield Scott, commander in chief of the United States Army, had picked up sixteen votes for the presidential nomination in the last Whig convention, he had so far had to remain in Washington at Polk's orders. Because Polk did not have a fully qualified and experienced Democratic general at his disposal—and because he did not want Taylor to gain any more spectacular national acclaim—he finally decided to appoint Winfield Scott to command the expedition which was to be sent to Veracruz.

Winfield Scott was then sixty-one years old but still vigorous, a towering man more than six feet four inches tall, and a good general. He had made a splendid record in the War of 1812, not only in training and organizing troops but as a hard-fighting leader who was always in the thick of combat. At the Battle of Lundy's Lane he was wounded so severely that he believed

Colonel Alexander W. Doniphan

Commodore John D. Sloat

Commodore Robert F. Sto

his military career was ended. "Old Fuss and Feathers" they called him now, for he was a stickler for military etiquette and discipline and loved full dress uniforms. In army blue, epaulets and buttons glistening, a yellow sash around his waist, he was a most imposing-looking general, a startling contrast to Old Rough and Ready.

Many of the troops Scott assembled at Tampico to board transports of the fleet bound for Veracruz came from Taylor's army. As part of his attempt to keep Taylor from getting a great deal of national publicity for his military exploits, President Polk was determined that he should not command a large army. Almost all of Taylor's regulars were detached—some four thousand men—with as many volunteers. He was left with fewer than five thousand men, all volunteers except for two squadrons of dragoons and several flying batteries.

Back home General Taylor's September victory at Monterrey was still being celebrated with a song.

> Old Zach's at Monterrey.
>   Bring on your Santa Anner.
> For every time we raise a gun,
>   Down goes a Mexicaner.

The second line of the song soon came true. Santa Anna, who had regained his power, was about to arrive at a critical time and point. News of Scott's expedition leaked out through the newspapers. An American dispatch, captured by the enemy, revealed to Santa Anna that Taylor's force had been gravely depleted. Here was a great opportunity for the Mexican general to smash one weakened army before a second could threaten him from the coast.

In February, 1847, Santa Anna, with 15,000 men, rapidly marched north. He advanced to the attack at Buena Vista. Old Rough and Ready, as rough as ever but not so ready, formed up his 4,800 men to meet the enemy.

American control of the Far West was established quickly by a number of resourceful leaders. Doniphan, who had marched to Santa Fe with Kearny, set out with his own force of 900 men and subdued and held the rest of New Mexico. Sloat launched the naval assault on California with his small squadron of ships; Stockton, who carried on for Sloat, threw his sailors into land combat that gained control of southern California. And it was Frémont, with his little band of sixty men, who began to establish American control of northern California.

ohn Charles Frémont

95

Buena Vista

In this Chamberlain painting General Zachary Taylor, riding the faithful Old Whitey, is shown in the thick of things at the Battle of Buena Vista. Taylor, never content to sit in his tent, insisted upon supervising the battle on the field, despite the danger.

At Buena Vista—which means beautiful view—lofty mountains were the backdrop for the high valley through which a road ran north from San Luis Potosí toward Saltillo. The road emerged by a narrow defile onto a broad plateau of fine fighting ground. Sloping ridges were the wings of this theater of warfare; few others in American history have possessed a setting of such grandeur.

Santa Anna came marching up the valley to find the bulk of the American force under General John E. Wool posted in a V-formation with its right wing covering the road and defending the pass. Taylor, with other troops, was at Saltillo, three miles south of Buena Vista hacienda. On swept the Mexicans, seizing a ridge. Lancers swung wide around the American left to swoop down toward Saltillo and strike the rear.

It was February 22, 1847—Washington's birthday, an occasion for the United States Army to celebrate with a victory if one could be gained by volunteers against Santa Anna's best, with odds of three to one in favor of the Mexicans.

American riflemen and Captain Braxton Bragg's battery beat back the enemy assaulting columns. The strains of "Hail Columbia," played by their bands, were ringing in their ears, along with the day's watchword, "Honor to Washington." Wool's men were still holding the line when darkness called a halt to the combat. Both armies shivered through a night of rain.

This 1846 picture of General Wool (probably the officer at front center) and his staff at Saltillo is one of the first daguerreotypes ever taken of American soldiers in wartime.

Next day Santa Anna massed his strength for an all-out assault. With his array marshaled rank on rank, bands struck up sacred music for a service. Priests in splendid robes burned incense and bestowed blessings on kneeling soldiers. In his book *The War with Mexico* the American historian Justin Smith included this description of the massing of Santa Anna's troops: "Evolution followed evolution. Eminence beyond eminence bristled with steel. All the colors of the rainbow—red, green, yellow, crim-son, sky-blue, turkey-blue—clothed the troops. Even the horses appeared to be in uniform, for those of a corps were alike in color. Silken banners and plumes of many bright hues floated on the breeze. Handsomely dressed aides dashed from point to point. Tremendous *vivas* rolled in mighty echoes from the mountains."

It was immensely impressive as a spectacle and as a display of military might. Many an American officer and soldier watched it gravely. The Americans did not lose their sense of humor, however. A Mississippi rifleman grinned and remarked that those lancers yonder in their bright-colored uniforms looked "too pretty to shoot." General Taylor, dressed as usual like a farmer, was even less bothered by the gorgeous array. He rode forward, halted, and scanned it. Hooking one leg over the pommel of Old Whitey's saddle, he snapped out orders to meet the forthcoming attack.

Two flying batteries opened on a dense Mexican column launched at the American center. The column seemed to dissolve and sink into the ground. Then two full enemy divisions poured down onto the plateau. With bands blaring their national anthem, they advanced at a steady parade step. A storm of shells and the withering fire of the Second Indiana Regiment shattered the van. They re-formed and came on again. The Indianans, though they had taken heavy casualties, stood fast till their colonel shouted, "Cease fire—retreat." They stumbled back, then broke and ran. One American cannon was lost; the rest of the battery was barely saved. Galloping lancers pursued the fugitives. In the nick of time American cavalry cut in, beat them off, and stemmed the rout.

Enemy shells ploughed into American ranks. Up on a ridge fluttered a flag blazoned with the arms of Mexico, the figure of St. Patrick, and a harp. Beneath it, the San Patricio Battalion of American deserters loaded their 18- and 24-pounder guns at top speed, hurling metal at their onetime com-

Captain Braxton Bragg—pictured above when he was a Confederate general in the Civil War—commanded a battery in the Battle of Buena Vista that delivered the death blow to Mexican defenses on February 23, 1847.

It is likely that the above daguerreotype of Zachary Taylor was taken when he was President of the United States (1849-50). The hero of the Mexican War was to have his term of office cut short by his death in 1850.

99

rades. Yet the Americans kept on
fighting and drove the enemy back
into the mountains. General Santa
Anna, his horse shot under him, was
carried along in the receding waves.

From another quarter, lancers
charged again, a galloping tide of flying manes and wind-swept pennons.

Now a storm broke over the mountains. Thunder pealed, drowning the
sound of the guns. Through the rain
Mexican officers, hands upraised to
ask safe conduct, rode up to General
Taylor. Santa Anna would like to be

informed on the American demands,
they said. General Wool was sent forward under a white flag to see if surrender was being offered. Soon he was
back, fired on by enemy guns. The
whole affair had been a trick to gain a
respite for the Mexicans and let them
muster strength for another effort.

Out from a ravine a Mexican corps
poured and struck powerfully. Bullets
could not halt it. Only three light cannon, spraying canister, had any effect.
The cannon were called "Bulldogs" by
Lieutenant John Paul Jones O'Brien,

In this charge in the Battle of Buena Vista the American dragoons (left), sabers swinging, cut their way through the onrushing ranks of skilled Mexican lancers (right). American cavalry horses, heavier than the Mexican mounts, proved sturdier in charges.

One gun was knocked out. O'Brien replaced it with another from reserve.

If the guns were not to be captured, it was time to retreat. Though all the horses of the limber teams had been killed, the pieces might still have been dragged off by hand. But, O'Brien thought, if he saved his guns the battle might be lost. He stayed and fought on. At last, the Mexicans overran the smoking cannon. O'Brien, badly wounded, limped away with the surviving members of his crews. A torrent of Mexicans, shouting wild *vivas*, swept forward in a victorious tide.

Illinois and Kentucky regiments tried to rally but were broken. Then forward on the run came the Third Indiana and the Mississippi Rifles, led by Colonel Jefferson Davis. The future president of the Confederacy was wounded and swaying in his saddle, but on he rode. They crashed into the Mexican right flank and rear.

General Taylor sat his white horse calmly watching while enemy fire was concentrated on him. One bullet ripped through the front of his coat, another tore his left sleeve. Near him the guns of flying batteries unlimbered and went into action. They were Bragg's and some of Thomas W. Sherman's, which had been rushed

who commanded them. The Mexican infantry, supported by artillery, rushed the Bulldogs, taking their losses and firing low and true. They overran O'Brien's 4-pounder, its crew strewn dead around it.

Almost surrounded, out in front, O'Brien kept blazing away with his two 6-pounders. When they fired and recoiled, cannoneers could not roll them back into position, for the enemy was too close. Cannoneers followed the recoiling pieces back, flung themselves on them, loaded and fired again.

over from the other end of the line.

Taylor called to Bragg, "What ammunition are you firing, Captain?"

"Canister, sir," the battery commander answered.

"Double or single?"

"Single, sir."

"Then double it and give 'em hell!"

Bragg did. Round after round of ammunition raked the Mexican ranks at short range. They wilted under the devastating blast. It was more than Santa Anna's men could endure. Spent, they reeled back over heaps of slain. The mountains swallowed their retreating columns. Not until the following day were the Americans aware of their victory over the Mexicans.

An American officer, weary from desperate combat with Mexican lancers, woke from a deep sleep the morning after the battle. He was Lew Wallace, who would one day pen the stirring novel *Ben-Hur*.

"The Mexican fires burned dim, and most of them were entirely out," Wallace wrote in a letter home. "I could hear no noise, but thought I could discover a cloud of dust far up the road. I could not then hope they were gone. I stood upon the breastwork, looking out keenly—day broke— it grew gradually lighter. I looked to the foot of the mountain at Battery No. 3 and thought I could see the dim outlines of the column that rested there at dark the night before. The light increased and I saw what I had taken for a column to be a row of palmetto. I looked up the road and saw distinctly the dust of their retreating column. Oh, what a feeling of relief came over me. I set up a shout of *victory*. It was a mockery, however. I had the day before felt very much as I should suppose a *whipped* man would feel—and I've

The island fortress of San Juan de Ulúa (center) guarded the harbor of the key Mexican port of Veracruz (background). The fleet carrying General Scott's army, seen anchored at the far left, arrived on March 9, 1847.

no doubt—had it been just as convenient for us as for Santa Anna to *vamos* [get out] we would have been off for Monterrey."

The army of "Old Wooden Leg," as the Americans called Santa Anna, had been beaten. It had been a close battle. Mexican losses—591 killed, 1,049 wounded, and 1,854 missing—had been twice the Americans'. Yet it might have been the other way around or worse, with the United States forces in the north all but destroyed and Scott's expedition compelled to return to protect the border.

Zachary Taylor lacked the strength to pursue the foe. He took no further part in the war, but the prestige of the Buena Vista victory made him the next President of the United States.

Two weeks later a fleet with General Scott's army aboard anchored off Veracruz where guns frowned from the ramparts of its coastal fortress.

From Veracruz to Cerro Gordo

Stormy seas tossed the American fleet of two hundred ships bound for Veracruz with nearly fourteen thousand troops aboard. Most of the larger ships weathered the rough seas, but forty smaller vessels, carrying many of the expedition's horses and mules,

sank. Some of the crews were saved when they took to the boats, but the animals that were penned in the holds were drowned.

General Scott, splendidly uniformed, stood on the bridge of his transport as it sailed into the outer harbor of Veracruz. Guns on the castle ramparts flamed, and a big shell narrowly missed the General's ship. It was a close call for the commander and his leading staff officers. If the gunners' aim had been a trifle better, the invasion would have been crippled at the very outset.

Signal flags fluttered from yardarms. They read: stand by to land troops. The landing was not easy. Transports were too numerous to crowd into the sea space before the landing area, so the soldiers were transferred to warships. By steam or sail the laden vessels moved as close to the beachhead as they could. Soldiers, weighted down with arms, ammunition, two days' rations, and water canteens, swarmed down the sides into surf boats.

A signal gun boomed on Scott's headquarters ship. Crews bent to their oars. The long line of boats dashed through the breakers and rollers for the shore. Now the Mexican commander might have shattered the crowded craft with artillery. The heavy guns of Veracruz, however, were more than two miles from the landing beach and did no damage. Only cavalry was at hand to oppose the landing. Shells from American gunboats drove them

back, and a flight of war rockets sent them galloping off in panic.

As the landing parties waded ashore, rifles and ammunition held high, and won their beachhead they raised the flag. Bands with the fleet struck up "The Star-Spangled Banner." Sand and soil began to fly from shovels while gun emplacements were built under the direction of an able young officer of the Corps of Engineers, Captain Robert E. Lee. General Scott's confidence in him would increase through the coming campaign and the following years. In fact, when the Civil War commenced Scott would offer him command of the United States Army. But Lee, giving his loyalty to his seceded state, Virginia, would refuse the post. Instead he would come to head the Confederate Army of Northern Virginia and lead it in brilliant victories, only surrendering

The American shore battery (opposite) is one of several fortifications that Captain Robert E. Lee designed for the bombardment of Veracruz. Mexican guerrilla fighters like the man at right—painted in 1833—slipped behind the American lines during the siege of Veracruz, taking shots at the enemy whenever they could get close enough to do so.

it after four years of bloody warfare.

Scott borrowed six heavy naval guns and their crews from Commodore Matthew C. Perry, who a few years later would open Japan to the western world. Those three 68-pounders and three long 32's were landed and dragged by manpower into position in pits behind parapets. Later they were joined by army siege cannon, including 10-inch mortars which could fling shells in a high arc over the battlements of Veracruz to burst within the city.

Some of Winfield Scott's officers, who had stormed Monterrey with Taylor, were impatient because an assault was not ordered at once. Scott was a cautious general, however, and would not risk the lives of several thousand soldiers in a direct assault.

So Captain Lee was allowed to finish his work, and meanwhile the siege lines were extended to surround the city. The Mexican commander had earlier been sent word that he could send women, children, and neutrals out of Veracruz to safety, but he had made no move to do so. It was too late now. No longer could the Americans delay, for the yellow fever season was approaching. The city must be captured and the army marched into higher, healthier country, or its ranks would be thinned by sickness.

Lee mounted a small white horse, not much larger than a pony, which he had bought in Tampico as a present for his youngest son and would later send home to the boy. The sturdy little

General Winfield Scott, the elegantly-uniformed Old Fuss and Feathers, sat for this portrait in 1851, looking as warlike as he must have looked when he arrived at Veracruz.

animal, which had been named Santa Anna, came in handy now, since the officer's two chargers had not yet arrived. He rode around the gun emplacements on an inspection, then reported to General Scott that the batteries were ready. Crews of the big siege pieces were ordered to fire.

With an awful roar the bombardment opened. Three hundred cannon on the ramparts of the city and castle made a furious reply. American casualties were light, however, despite the heavy bombardment. Most of the enemy projectiles, flinging up geysers of sand, buried themselves harmlessly in the parapets of Lee's well-protected batteries, or fell wide of the target. It was a different story inside the city of Veracruz. Huge shells crashed through walls and burst in the streets. To one listening soldier the mortar bombs in flight sounded like hungry lions howling for their prey. Roofs collapsed, and houses were set afire. Bells in steeples, their ropes untouched, clanged wildly from the blows of steel fragments. The shrieks and wails of the dying and wounded were carried by the wind to the American lines. Faces turned grave with pity, for some of those hit must be women and children who could have been sent to safety.

Through three days and nights the bombardment thundered. Hissing rockets traced a red path through the dark skies. At last, when most of the Mexican batteries had been silenced and a whole quarter of the city leveled, a white flag fluttered from the ramparts. The Mexicans, their losses 180 soldiers and civilians killed and many wounded, surrendered. Veracruz had been captured at the cost of one hundred American casualties, of whom nineteen were killed.

The castle and town were patrolled by American troops, and the Navy guarded the port for shipments of supplies while its marines joined Scott's force. On April 8 the army marched, driving for the heart of the enemy's domain—Mexico City.

Veracruz receded behind Scott's marching men. The sun shimmered on its walls, on the sea, and the hulls of naval vessels at anchor. Blazing heat tormented the columns, heat that would soon bring the dreaded fever that yellowed the skins of its victims as they sickened and died. Still the endless sand hills surrounded the marchers, and their legs were scratched by the prickly chaparral bushes that grew in the sandy soil.

The march was slow down the road the old Spaniards had built from the coast through to Mexico City. The first stretch of the road, fallen in disrepair, was "sandier than New Jersey," said soldiers from that state. Scott's three divisions—8,500 men—struggled along. Only a few transport animals had arrived by sea or been collected by raids on the countryside. Artillery and cavalry moved at a snail's pace, sparing such horses as they had. To save the strength of supply wagon and pack mules, baggage had been cut to a minimum. It was still scorching hot. Some soldiers, exhausted and sick, straggled away and lay down in the brush. Following troops came upon their hacked bodies. Hovering Mexican guerrillas had finished them off.

Somewhere ahead they must meet the foe in force. In fact, Santa Anna, falsely reporting that he had won a victory at Buena Vista, had hastened down from the north. With first-rate generalship he had brought his army, which had stood up well under forced marches, to the defense of the approaches to the Mexican capital. Now with 12,000 troops he barred the path of the oncoming Americans.

For Scott's marching men the air gradually freshened when they began climbing into the mountains. They felt they had left the tropics and reached

the temperate zone. Where the National Road cut through mountain heights, peaks frowned down on it—Cerro Gordo, Atalaya, and others. Cerro Gordo, the Big Hill, would give its name to the important battle that lay ahead. The pass it dominated was 4,260 feet above sea level.

Santa Anna had defended that pass with troops. Theirs was a position altogether formidable, but the Americans had to press on to Mexico City.

Scott's army halted and deployed. Direct assault could be as costly as it would have been at Veracruz. Some other means, such as a flank attack, must be found. Several young officers were called to headquarters and ordered to scout the ground. One of them was Captain Lee.

Daringly Lee made his way around the enemy left and into the rear. He

The cartoon above makes fun of the flight of Santa Anna (left) and General Valentín Canalizo after the Mexican defeat at Cerro Gordo on April 18, 1847. The defeat was especially humiliating for Santa Anna, who was then both commander of Mexico's army and, for the second time, president of Mexico.

Inside Veracruz (left) panic reigned when the Americans unleashed the full force of their bombardment on March 25, 1847. Although casualty rates in the city were not huge, many civilians as well as soldiers died.

was near a spring when he caught a glimpse of several Mexican soldiers coming through the woods for a drink. At once he dropped prone behind a fallen log. For hours he lay still in his hiding place. Insects stung him; he could not risk brushing them off or scratching. The slightest move or noise would have betrayed him, and he would probably have been bayoneted or shot. Soldiers walked over, sat down on the very log that concealed him and held long conversations, while Lee scarcely dared breathe. It was dark before traffic to the spring ceased. Lee got stiffly to his feet and groped back to the American lines with the vital information he had gained. He had discovered a route to outflank the foe.

Next day he guided troops back over it. Pioneers, troops of the Corps of Engineers, hewed a path through

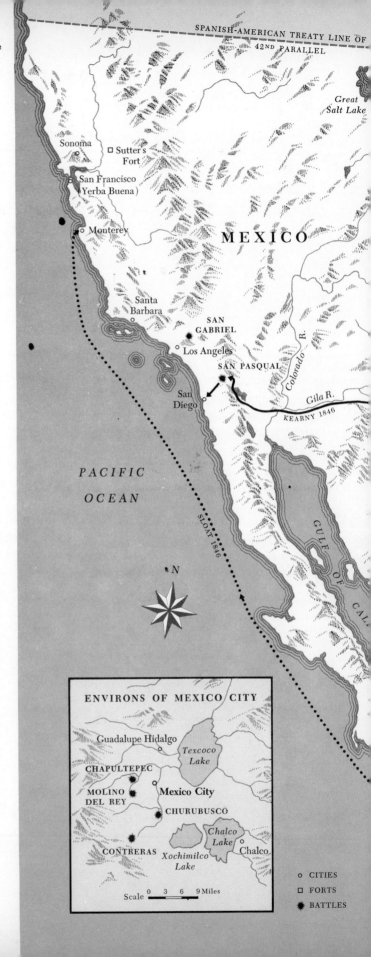

The United States had to plan its strategy well in fighting a war with Mexico. The land area of Mexico was an enormous territory to bring under military control; and the spirited Mexican army was capable of making the task very difficult for the Americans. The initial strategy of the United States was the four-pronged attack on Mexico already outlined on page 71. There were, however, many complications that altered the original plan of attack; for the battle strategy had to be reshaped each time the enemy made an unexpected move. The four original American attacks—led by Taylor, Wool, Kearny, and Scott—are shown on the map at right, along with other important attacks and advances. Sloat sailed from the important Mexican port of Mazatlán for Monterey on June 8, 1846, to begin his phase of the over-all attack. He had put in at Mazatlán because there were American diplomatic agents there who were in a position to tell him when it was certain that full-scale war had broken out. The most vital military target in all Mexico was the country's heart — its beautiful capital, Mexico City. The inset map shows the battles that led to the capture of Mexico City; when it fell, the nation fell.

CAMPAIGNS AND BATTLES
OF THE MEXICAN WAR
INCLUDING THE TEXAS WAR FOR INDEPENDENCE

Fort
Leavenworth

Missouri R.

KEARNY 1846

MISSOURI

Bent's
Fort

Arkansas R.

ARKANSAS

Taos

Santa
Fe   Las Vegas

TEXAS BOUNDARY AS CLAIMED BY MEXICO AFTER 1836

Red R.

Mississippi R.

MISSISSIPPI

VALVERDE

TEXAS

(ADMITTED 1845)

Pecos R.

Colorado R.

Brazos R.

Sabine R.

LOUISIANA

EL BRAZITO

El Paso

TEXAS BOUNDARY AS CLAIMED BY TEXAS AFTER 1836

Austin

Washington

New
Orleans

San
Antonio   San Felipe
Gonzales 1835

SAN JACINTO
1836

Presidio
del Norte

Rio Grande

ALAMO
1836

Goliad
(La Bahia) 1835

SCOTT 1846

SACRAMENTO

Chihuahua

Presidio
de Rio Grande

Nueces R.

Refugio

San
Patricio

Corpus
Christi

Laredo

DONIPHAN 1847

Monclova

WOOL 1846

Mier

Fort
Brown

Matamoros

TAYLOR 1846-47

Saltillo   MONTERREY

Parras

BUENA
VISTA

QUITMAN 1846

MEXICO

Salado

Cedral

PATTERSON 1847

Mazatlán

Pánuco R.

San Luis
Potosí

Tampico

SCOTT 1847

GULF OF

MEXICO

Scale

0   100   150 Miles

Mexico
City   Perote   Jalapa

Puebla   VERACRUZ

CERRO
GORDO

PALO
ALTO   Point
Isabel

RESACA
DE LA PALMA

Fort
Brown

Rio Grande

Gulf of Mexico

Matamoros

PALO ALTO AND
RESACA DE LA PALMA

Scale   0   3   6   9 Miles

The picture above shows Scott's army assembled at Cerro Gordo for the battle against Santa Anna's troops. The Americans won a decisive victory at Cerro Gordo despite rugged and treacherous terrain — and despite setbacks in strategy. This victory opened the road to Mexico City to the American army; the final battles of the war lay ahead.

the forest and brush for artillery following the infantry. Ravines too deep for any gun team to cross confronted them. Horses were unhitched and driven down into them and up the steep opposite slopes, climbing like cats. The cannon, no light pieces but heavy 24-pounders, were lowered by ropes to the bottom, then hoisted up the other side by straining crews. Still unsus-

swung along it toward his left. And still the Mexicans, guarding the passes, were unaware of the deadly threats poised on flank and rear. Only a few more hours were needed for the spearhead troops to move into assault positions and wait there in concealment through the night of April 17, 1847, as General Scott had ordered. Next morning they would strike with the weight of the rest of the army behind them.

But the flanking force was led by blustering General Daniel E. Twiggs. He was called "the Bengal Tiger," but though he could roar loudly, there the resemblance ended. Unlike the great beast that creeps up on its prey and pounces at the right moment, Twiggs pushed his column ahead without caution. Captain Lee asked him to halt while pioneers raised a brush screen in front of a gap in the trees, a gap open to enemy observation. Twiggs refused and marched on. From a peak the Mexicans spotted the blue American uniforms in the gap and rushed forward to seize a hill that had been unoccupied. Twiggs, having thrown away the great advantage of surprise, tried to storm the hill. Ninety men were killed or wounded in that rash attempt.

Santa Anna, warned now of the menace to his left, shifted troops and cannon to meet it. At sunrise on the eighteenth his bugles blared a challenge. The American guns and the rocket battery, which had been hoisted up to the summit of Atalaya, answered with bursts of fire. Infantry surged forward all along the line. Again the im-

pected by the enemy, the flanking force reached its position for the attack on Cerro Gordo. Later on, by a similar mighty effort, guns would be hauled up to a vantage point on the summit of Atalaya.

Now the American strength was mustered for the crucial attack. One force thrust forward over Lee's route to fall on the enemy's rear. Another

patient Twiggs blundered. Before the attack on the Mexican rear could develop, he flung part of his own command against a steep, fortified height. Colonel William S. Harney's saber flashed as he led the Seventh Infantry and the First Artillery, fighting as infantrymen, against the palisades at the foot of the slope. With equal bravery the Mexican defenders met them, first with a hail of bullets, then bayonet to bayonet. The American troops broke through and swept on upward over clumps of spiked cactus. They burst through an abatis, a tough barrier of interlaced tree branches and brush. Finally tall Harney took them over a stone wall on the crest, and the hill was won. Down from a tower staff slid the red, white, and green flag of Mexico. The American flag was raised in its place.

It was then, with fugitives streaming back in retreat from the high ground, that General Shields's brigade struck the Mexican rear.

"The *Yanquis!* They've come out on the road!" the startled Mexicans yelled.

For a time cannon held off the blue attack but not for long. Though Shields fell severely wounded, his men overran the guns and turned them on the enemy. Two thousand Mexican cavalrymen, posted to guard the road, wheeled and fled. Panic spread. Everywhere rose the desperate cry, "Save yourself if you can!"

While Santa Anna vainly strove to stem the rout, his carriage was caught in the jam. The one-legged general had been using it to spare himself the difficulty of horseback riding. Hemmed in, the Mexican leader was close to capture by onrushing Americans. An aide cut the traces of one of the carriage mules and helped Santa Anna to mount it and gallop to safety.

Illinois troops swarmed over the carriage. One soldier whooped as he found a prized souvenir—Santa Anna's cork leg. Others discovered a sack of gold coins which they turned over to the army pay chest. Consciences clear, they settled for a roast chicken, the General's lunch, as their share.

The battle raged on as victorious Americans dashed forward in an attempt to cut off the fleeing Mexican army. But many Mexican troops, disorganized though they were, stampeded out over the avenue of escape before it could be closed.

General Scott, riding forward, sat his charger "under a canopy of balls" as fearlessly as Taylor. Tears of pride and joy ran down the cheeks of the old warrior while he watched his men break the last enemy resistance and rush on in pursuit. A smashing victory had been won. American losses were 417; the Mexicans', more than 1,000, with 3,000 taken prisoner. Many more would have been captured if Twiggs's premature attacks had not betrayed surprise and left the road uncut long

This 1847 print shows one of the encounters in hand-to-hand combat of Mexican and American troops in the last phase of the furious battle of Cerro Gordo on April 18, 1847.

enough for the escape of two thirds of the opposing army.

Forty-three cannon and 4,000 small arms, ammunition, supplies, and a pay chest containing $11,000 in silver were among the spoils taken after the Battle of Cerro Gordo.

On the battlefield the wounded were picked up and carried to field hospitals. Captured Mexican surgeons, helping the American doctors, noted that their own men were as carefully handled as those who wore blue uniforms and that they had been given drinks from the canteens of soldiers who only a short time before had faced them in combat. Word filtered further through Mexico that American treatment of enemy wounded and prisoners was humane. While Santa Anna's lancers had been known to spear American wounded, and his guerrillas mercilessly slaughtered foragers and stragglers, he had not revived the no quarter order of the Alamo and Goliad. This war was waged as fiercely but less bitterly than the one for Texas independence.

When Scott's army marched on to Jalapa, the crowds lining the streets were neither unfriendly nor afraid.

On August 7, 1847, General Winfield Scott's army (above) began to move out of its base at Puebla. Scott was headed for Mexico City, and neither rough roads like the one shown in this painting nor the Mexican army's superior number of troops could discourage him.

The Battle of
Contreras

Camped on the high ground around Jalapa, Scott's army was free from the greatly feared yellow fever of the low, hot coastal regions. (It was not discovered until after the Spanish-American War that the fever was carried by mosquitoes which bred in the swamps of the lowlands.) Yet the sick list swelled, and the hospitals filled. It was cool, even cold, in the mountain country. New uniforms to replace those worn out in the campaign did not come through, nor did money enough to pay troops and purchase provisions. Supply wagons broke down, and their mules died in harness on the long, hard pull from Veracruz. Because the poorly fed troops ate too many oranges, plums, and other fruits, there were frequent cases of dysentery. Though many of the soldiers recovered, there were also many men so weakened by the disease that they died.

Once more disease, not battle, was the great killer of armies, as it had been throughout history and would continue to be until the advance of medical science reversed the scale in the Second World War. In the war with Mexico, estimates of total American losses were from 1,500 to 1,700 killed and wounded, with deaths from disease 6,000 to 11,000.

The army's strength was further sapped when General Scott was compelled to send home seven regiments of volunteers whose enlistment time had almost expired. To hold them any longer would have exposed them to an increasing risk of yellow fever when they marched to Veracruz to embark. Now the Americans, occupying Jalapa and later Puebla, dwindled to 5,820 men, deep in hostile territory, while the Mexican force menacing them was rated at 7,000 regulars and 15,000 national guardsmen. When the Duke of Wellington in England was told the situation he exclaimed, "Scott is lost! He has been carried away by his successes. He can't take the city, and he can't fall back upon [Veracruz]."

Far from considering himself lost, Scott believed he stood on the threshold of victory. Given the reinforcements and supplies he asked, he was confident he could achieve it. President Polk in Washington had different ideas. Two Whig generals had been winning the war, and that might lose the next election for the Democrats.

Peace negotiations now might recapture much of the credit for the Administration. Therefore Polk sent a State Department official, Nicholas P. Trist, to Mexico to negotiate a treaty.

Scott quarreled bitterly and openly with Trist over the methods he planned to use with Santa Anna but finally fell in with Trist's scheme of paying a sum of money to persuade Santa Anna to acknowledge defeat. The negotiations with Santa Anna are described in the following passage from the Department of the Army's publication *American Military History 1607-1953*. "The Mexican President agreed that for $10,000 down and $1,000,000 to be paid when a treaty was ratified he would discuss peace terms. After the down payment was safely in hand, however, Santa Anna discovered that he could not prevail upon the Mexican Congress to repeal a law it had passed making it high treason for any official to treat with the Americans. It was clear that Scott would have to move closer to the capital of Mexico before Santa Anna would seriously consider terms . . ."

In June, 1847, several thousand troops and a large convoy of supplies arrived from the coast. August brought still more reinforcements under General Franklin Pierce, a future President of the United States—2,500 soldiers, all of them raw except for a detachment of marines; also a battery of siege guns. Scott's strength was raised to 14,000 men, but 2,500 of them were sick, and 600 of the earlier invalids were still much too weak to march.

It was already August, and to Scott it seemed that he could not delay his attack any longer. Leaving a small garrison at Puebla, he cut loose from his base. If he left troops to guard the road back to Veracruz, his army would not be strong enough to advance. With great daring, he had taken a grave risk. One battle lost would mean that he and his army were lost as well, as the Duke of Wellington had predicted.

The long blue column formed: dragoons, infantry, and artillery, and supply wagons and the new ambulance that had recently come. General Scott galloped its length, each regimental band playing "Hail to the Chief." He was ready to march on Mexico City.

Mexico City, prize of battle, lay surrounded by lakes in its high valley 7,000 feet above sea level. Guarding the approaches to the city with his troops, Santa Anna was determined to prevent the United States army from reaching the city itself.

Fortified hills, villages, and other obstacles defended all four roads to the capital. Scott, choosing to advance toward its western gate, halted his troops in mid-march. Frontal assault down a highway would cost too high a "butcher's bill" as soldiers called the list of killed and wounded—too great a price for a general careful of the lives of his men to be willing to pay. Some route around the enemy's flank and into his rear must be found.

Again the invaluable Captain Lee was given the task. He began to circle

The 1847 sketch above, made by an officer who served in many Mexican War campaigns, shows American troops crossing a steep mountain during the war. The battles at Cerro Gordo and Contreras were fought in country like this. Cannons were hoisted up the mountain with ropes, as discussed on page 112.

the Mexican right until he was confronted by the Pedregal, a lava bed
spread by the eruptions of volcanoes
long ago. An expanse fifteen miles
square, just southwest of Mexico
City, it was a forbidding barrier of
jagged rocks, so sharp they cut boots,
and a network of crevices that would

break the legs of horses that stepped
into them. But a mule path ran over
it, evidence that it had been crossed
and could be crossed again, at least by
infantry in single file. If it was im-
proved by a road, artillery could man-
age it. Lee and his escort, following
the path, were driven back by the fire

of a Mexican picket. Yet he reported in favor of an attack over the Pedregal in spite of its difficulties and the fact that it was defended. Engineers and infantrymen started to build the road, and troops moved up into position.

The Battle of Contreras or Padierna, August 19 and 20, 1847, somewhat re-

On August 19, 1847, American troops launched the first major attack of the Battle of Contreras. Troops under the command of General Gideon Pillow attacked the forces of General Gabriel Valencia, whose camp near Contreras appears in the background. The mounted officer at right is probably Pillow.

Ulysses S. Grant   *George B. McClellan*   *George G. Meade*

These three West Point graduates who fought gallantly in the Mexican War were to achieve lasting fame as Union officers in the Civil War. Grant was to be President of the United States.

sembled Cerro Gordo. Again there was a premature attack, this time by General Gideon J. Pillow, whose men were routed by the Mexicans, fighting with great gallantry. American artillery was almost blasted out of its positions. For a time it was touch and go.

Sometimes the outcome of a battle depends chiefly upon one man. Scott's was the generalship, but most of his decisions were based on the reports of Captain Robert E. Lee. After that first reconnaissance, Lee repeatedly recrossed the Pedregal, guiding troops and bringing batteries into action. During the night of the nineteenth, in one of those raging thunderstorms which so often punctuated battles in the mountains of Mexico, he made the perilous passage twice, carrying vital orders when seven other officers had failed to get through. Most of the time he was on foot, since the ground was usually too dangerous for riding.

Though without sleep for thirty-six hours, his iron endurance survived the ordeal. Almost every general on the field paid him glowing tributes.

At last General Persifor Smith's infantry, followed by the battery of Captain Simon Drum, Fourth Artillery, burst into the Mexican rear. Other soldiers in blue, rushing in from Padierna, clamped the foe like the second jaw of a vise. Crushed, Santa Anna's army went to pieces. Fleeing lancers rode down a screaming mob of infantry, camp women, and laborers. A stampeding herd of mules heightened the chaos. Only two 6-pounder guns held their ground and kept firing. Their cannoneers were said to have been chained to the cannon to prevent them from deserting their posts.

Those two bronze cannons looked familiar to Captain Drum. He was certain they were O'Brien's Bulldogs, captured at the Battle of Buena Vista,

Robert E. Lee

Thomas J. Jackson

Jefferson Davis

The three West Pointers above fought beside the men on the opposite page in the Mexican War and fought against them in the Civil War; all three were to become famous Confederate leaders.

brought down from the north and here manned in desperation. Drum shouted for his battery to limber up and charged at a gallop. A volley swept his guidon-bearer from the saddle, but a lieutenant caught the flag as it fell. The column crashed into the Mexican position. Vaulting from his mount, Drum laid hands on the guns O'Brien had lost at Buena Vista.

Today you may see those very guns at the U.S. Military Academy at West Point. A plaque beside them reads:

O'BRIEN

LOST WITHOUT
DISHONOR AT THE BATTLE
OF BUENA VISTA, BY
A COMPANY OF THE
4TH ARTILLERY.
RECAPTURED WITH
JUST PRIDE AND
EXULTATION BY THE
SAME REGIMENT AT
CONTRERAS.
WINFIELD SCOTT

DRUM

That final swift and spirited attack had won the field in seventeen minutes. Twenty-two cannon, much ammunition, and many horses and mules were taken. About seven hundred Mexicans had been killed and another eight hundred captured, while the Americans had suffered only sixty casualties. Scott's army swung onto the road for the last lap to Mexico City. With it rolled a new battery, including those famous trophies, O'Brien's Bulldogs, and organized in their honor.

But still barring the way to the capital lay the fortified village of Churubusco and its strong-walled convent, bristling with guns. Their crews were the elite of the Mexican artillery, the San Patricio Battalion. The moment was near for the settlement of another account dating back to Monterrey and Buena Vista. Surely it would be settled in blood. The American deserters of the San Patricios would fight to the last.

On August 20, 1847, in the middle of the afternoon, the American attack on the convent of Churubusco (above) began to succeed. American troops, having fought their way through the outer defenses, were able to approach and breach the walls of the convent.

Churubusco:

Place of the War God

Press the pursuit, Scott ordered. Give the enemy no chance to reorganize and stand. Drive straight through to Mexico City if possible. In obedience, troops in blue surged forward.

But the Mexican army possessed an amazing ability to recover and rally even after a disastrous defeat. Holding Churubusco would grant them respite—would allow Santa Anna an opportunity to marshal his still considerable strength, 16,000 men, to protect the capital. So the general in chief and president of Mexico commanded the

On August 15, 1847, Santa Anna managed to have broadsides like the one above distributed behind the American lines. He hoped to encourage more American deserters; the San Patricios had been very helpful to him.

Following their standard bearer, the American troops in the picture above are fighting their way over the walls of the savagely defended Mexican tête-de-pont (bridgehead) at the approach to the convent of Churubusco.

hard core of veterans who were Churubusco's garrison to defend their post to the last man.

The Americans could have bypassed that fortified town. Yet if they did, they would leave behind them what is called in military terms a "hedgehog." Attacks like sharp quills from the animal could be launched from it against the invaders' rear. On August 20, 1847, Scott issued a new order: Storm Churubusco.

Churubusco, whose name was derived from an Aztec word meaning "place of the war god," would soon live up to its name. Assaults had to be delivered over a ditch-flanked causeway leading to a stone bridge across a river canal. Every inch of the approach could be swept by cannon fire. Beyond rose the massive walls of the Convent of San Pablo with its chapel and garden. It had been turned into a fort. And Americans would shortly be made aware of the grim fact that most of that formidable array of artillery was served by crack gunners, the San Patricios under ex-Sergeant Riley.

Famous old American regiments, with gallant records in the Revolution and in the War of 1812, advanced along the causeway. Deadly cannon fire swept them back. A deluge of solid cannon balls—round shot— poured down on them. From the muzzles of the Mexican guns burst deadly sprays of grapeshot—small iron balls clustered around a rod like a bunch of grapes on its stem—and of canister. The Mexican fire blew up two American caissons (ammunition wagons) with a roar and cut down gun crews. More artillerymen in blue were picked off by sharpshooters in a church tower.

The defenders at the bridgehead and their assailants were so close to each other that they were able to distinguish each others' faces through the battle smoke. The San Patricios, sighting along their gun barrels, recognized some of their former officers leading the assaulting troops. At the shortened ranges the expert gunners of the Red Company could use their cannon as sniping weapons. They loaded their guns with canister, aimed carefully, and fired.

The San Patricios were the backbone of the defense. Their deadly fire accounted for a large proportion of the considerable American losses which rose to 139 killed, 876 wounded, and forty missing. Santa Anna later declared: "Give me a few hundred more men like Riley's and I would have won the victory."

Again and again the Americans attacked and as often were flung back with heavy losses. Widened lines strove to close in on other sides of the stronghold, thrusting through the tall corn and wading the drainage ditches. Volleys and sorties by the garrison smashed them back.

Gradually stubborn American valor and keen marksmanship began to tell. One force made a circuit, forded a canal, and advanced to seize the road to the capital. Plainly it could not be checked for long. As it narrowed the avenues of escape, a trickle, then a stream of Mexicans commenced retreating while the way was still open.

The defenders of the stone bridge began to waver. American troops swarmed down on the bridge and stormed it at bayonet point. Mexican guns captured there were swung around to pound the walls of the convent. Breaches gaped in its masonry. The Mexican infantrymen in its garrison started to lower the colors and hoist the white flag of surrender. Before their hands could touch the halyards, knives were plunged into their backs by the San Patricios.

Grim Riley and his battalion of American deserters would allow their Mexican comrades neither to surrender nor to retreat. The San Patricios well knew that betrayal of their country had placed hangmen's nooses around their necks. Better die fighting than be taken prisoner and dangle from a gallows.

The breaches in the convent's defenses widened. The fire of the defenders, their ammunition dwindling, slackened. Cheering, Scott's assault columns crashed through into the convent garden.

Now a strange event raised the combat to the height of ferocity. Among the storming American troops was a unit called the Spy Company,

OVERLEAF: *The Mexican troops in this picture of about 1850 are staging a counterattack against the Americans trying to take Molino del Rey, seen at rear center, on September 8, 1847 (see description on pages 133-34).*

composed entirely of renegade Mexicans. Robbed or wronged in other ways by their own people, they had—like the San Patricios—joined the enemy and had proved as valuable as scouts to the Americans as Riley and his men had been to the Mexican artillery. So in the last clash in the convent traitors fought traitors, battling with hatred and fury. American infantry by the side of the Spy Company attacked the enemy just as mercilessly.

By tens and scores the San Patricios fell. A few managed to escape. At length, out of a battalion of 260, only Riley and seventy-four of his gunners were taken alive.

Santa Anna's army streamed away in flight, hotly pursued by American infantry and dragoons whose sabers slashed, cutting down fugitives. Captain Phil Kearny led two of the squadrons harrying the retreat. Though trumpets sounded the recall, he galloped on with two squads of his own gray horse troop whose mounts he had bought with his own money to assure their uniform color. On they rode, straight to a gate of Mexico City. As they burst through, a cannon blast mangled Kearny's left arm. His cavalrymen supported him, reeling in the saddle, while they wheeled and rode back. Kearny recovered, but his arm had to be amputated. A general in the Civil War, he rode with his reins in his teeth, his right arm wielding a saber. He met the death that had missed him in Mexico at Chantilly, Virginia, during the Civil War.

The American army gained a great victory at Churubusco. Four thousand Mexicans were killed or wounded; those casualties plus prisoners and other missing whittled down Santa Anna's strength by one third. Captures included eight generals and thirty-seven cannon. But the cost of victory was far from cheap for the Americans: 16 officers and 139 enlisted men were killed, while 60 officers and 816 rank-and-file were wounded.

But the last barrier on the road to Mexico City had been smashed.

The fate of the survivors of the San Patricio Battalion was soon determined. Eight-pound, 3-prong iron collars were riveted around their necks, and they were held under heavy guard for a court martial. In a fair trial they were convicted and given sentences that were strictly in accordance with the military laws of the period, though Mexicans fumed that the punishment was Gringo barbarism. Riley and others, who had deserted before the commencement of hostilities, were ordered to be whipped and branded. The remaining fifty San Patricios were condemned to be hanged for desertion in time of war.

Ex-Sergeant Riley, who was lashed and branded with a "D" for deserter, would labor as a convict as long as the army remained in Mexico. Then, head shaved and buttons stripped from the uniform he had dishonored, he was drummed out of camp while fifes piped the "Rogue's March."

One group of the deserters who had been condemned to death was executed soon after their trial. Riley and the others who had been spared were forced to dig their graves. Then the condemned men, nooses around their necks, were placed in carts which were driven out from under long gallows. The rest of the condemned men were held until the American army made its final assault on Mexico City.

Today in a suburb of Mexico City stands a cross in memory of the San Patricio Battalion. It is marked with a gamecock, symbol of their bravery— with dice, token of their gamble with fate—and with an emblem of the stake they risked: the skull and crossbones of death.

Chapultepec

During a two week armistice, Scott's and Santa Anna's armies girded themselves for the crucial struggle for Mexico City. The city—which was on a high plateau—was dominated by a hill; on the summit of the hill stood the Castle of Chapultepec. The palace of the Aztec emperor Montezuma had once stood on this same hill.

Mexico City in its formidable grandeur drew every eye in the American army. Lofty mountains ringed it— heights whose passes were threaded by highways to both coasts and to the north. Those roads led to the city gates over causeways, or embankments, raised above the swamps that surrounded the capital like the moat of a medieval stronghold. The castle and the governor's palace loomed above

The American soldiers above are fighting their way to the Castle of Chapultepec, looming in the background, above the battlefield. James Walker, who painted this panoramic canvas in 1857, probably based his work on sketches he made when the battle was in progress.

massive walls studded with cannon.

Over in the Castle of Chapultepec itself Mexican soldiers stood to arms. Part of its garrison consisted of cadets of the military academy it housed—about one hundred boys in their early teens or younger. In a gallant defense of the castle, many cadets would die.

Now American siege cannon, which are called battering guns, opened their fire, and Mexican artillery answered.

One of the outworks of the city, Molino del Rey (the King's Mill), was reported to be a foundry where cannon were being cast from church bells, and a quantity of powder was stored. On September 8, Scott ordered it taken.

His men advanced to the assault with the raw courage they had always shown, but they were not as well led

133

as usual. An American column, attempting to take the mill at bayonet point, did not give the American 24-pounders enough time to breach the walls of the mill and soften the Mexican defenses. The advancing American troops, therefore, were caught in extremely heavy Mexican fire from the mill; since they were right in the line of fire, their own 24-pounders could not be brought immediately back into action against the walls of the mill and the Mexican gun emplacements around the mill. All day long the combat raged until at last the Americans won Molino del Rey in hand-to-hand fighting.

Scott's force, shrunken now to 8,300, faced a foe estimated to number from 18,000 to 20,000 troops.

Yet the U. S. army must attack again and without delay. It must advance over the causeways and approach roads to the city as deadly as those at Churubusco had been. At the causeways' ends were gates to be burst in—narrow, barricaded streets to be cleared — garrisoned houses of the enemy's capital to be fought for, wall by wall, roof by roof. And two hundred feet above the plain loomed the citadel of Chapultepec to be stormed before victory could be won.

It was General John A. Quitman's

division that began the advance toward the heights of Chapultepec. Burly, red-bearded Quitman had been a Mississippi lawyer.

At eight o'clock on the morning of September 13, 1847, American siege guns fell suddenly silent. It was the signal for the assault. Spearhead columns thrust toward the castle and the city gates. They floundered through the clinging mud of cypress swamps. The going was tough and bloody.

The vanguard of the Fourteenth

The American troops at right are storming the walls of the Castle of Chapultepec on September 13, 1847. The men climbing up the scaling ladders are urged on by their standard bearer, holding the flag at center.

U. S. Infantry was swept from one causeway, as if by the strokes of an iron broom, under the furious fire of an enemy fieldpiece behind a sandbag barricade. A courier on a lathered horse dashed back with a plea for artillery support. Captain John Bankhead Magruder—"Prince John" the army called him—turned to a quiet, shy lieutenant. "Mister Jackson," he ordered, "take your section forward and clear the road."

Lieutenant Thomas Jonathan Jackson—who, as a general in the Civil War, came to be nicknamed "Stonewall" —led his two guns onward at a clattering gallop. One of them was blasted off the causeway. The second was unlimbered and prepared for action, though most of its crew was soon killed or wounded. Jackson and a sergeant manned it alone. They stood in the open and fought a close-range duel with the barricaded enemy cannon.

Now Magruder was up with the rest of the battery. He leaped from his

horse as it was shot under him, and his guns chimed in with Jackson's. Their shells deluged the Mexican piece. Infantry rushed it, and the way was open.

Flame ringed the outer defenses of the Castle of Chapultepec. A hail of iron poured down on the assaulting troops clambering up the rocky slopes. Over their heads thundered rounds from a long 18-pounder and an 8-inch howitzer, served by artillerymen under S. H. Drum and Calvin Benjamin. Shells pierced the walls and burst within them.

Steadily the Americans inched up the steep grades. They flooded over the outer breastworks and down into the fosse, or ditch, that surrounded the castle. Sheer walls towered above.

Where were the scaling ladders? They could have been quickly carried forward directly after the assault, but they had not yet arrived. Storm troops were penned in the ditch for fifteen or twenty dreadful minutes. They lived because Mexican cannon on the ramparts could not be depressed to reach them and because their own rifles

At a crucial moment in the Battle of Chapultepec, when the American position on the north side of the castle (above) was dangerously weakened, Lieutenant Thomas Jackson—with the aid of a sergeant—kept a single American cannon booming against the enemy. All of the flags at right flew in the Mexican War. The banner at top—taken in battle by American troops—is the national flag of Mexico; one like it flew from the staff of Chapultepec and every other Mexican fortress. The colors at center belonged to Company I of the Fourth Regiment of Indiana Volunteers. The flag at bottom, the colors of the United States Eighth Infantry Regiment, may well have been the first American banner to fly over Chapultepec after its fall.

An officer of the gallant Mexican San Blas Battalion that defended the foot of Chapultepec Hill was taken wounded from the field wrapped in his company's battle flag (above).

picked off every Mexican who showed himself on the parapets.

The ladders were on hand at last. They were instantly placed against the walls, and infantrymen swarmed up. Fire from below could not cover all the climbers. Ladders covered with soldiers were shoved back by the enemy and crashed to the ground.

A wave of men swept over the battlements— New Yorkers, South Carolinians, and Pennsylvanians. There were also the voltigeurs (light infantry sharpshooters) and the regiment of mounted riflemen that would win Scott's accolade of "the Brave Rifles"; Quitman's division with marines and pioneers heading it; and Worth's command with two young officers, future Confederate generals in its ranks — Longstreet and Pickett. Lieutenant James Longstreet, bearing the regimental colors, fell wounded. Lieutenant George Pickett — of Pickett's

Charge at Gettysburg—caught the flag and carried it on.

Within the castle walls the military academy cadets, in gray uniforms and blue tasseled caps, fought valiantly by the side of their older comrades. *Los Niños*—the boys—they were called, but it was a man's part they played that day. Their bravery built one of Mexico's most cherished traditions, for their memory is highly honored in Mexico today. *Los Niños* were the last defenders of the flag. When they had fallen, down came the banner of Mexico from its tall staff to be replaced by the white flag of surrender, and then by the American flag. At this very moment the remaining members of the San Patricios who had been condemned to death were hanged on scaffolds just outside the city—but within sight of the walls and the castle. In the moment before their execution, the condemned men cheered the flag they had betrayed.

The weary men who had captured Chapultepec gathered themselves to support the final attack on the city.

Inside the San Cosme Gate, battered in by Jackson, bayonets surged through the streets. For a time the fighting was as bitter as it had been at Monterrey. As the American commanders had expected, there were barricades in the streets and snipers on the house tops. Lieutenants U. S. Grant, Infantry, and Raphael Semmes, Navy (a volunteer aide to a general), mustered crews to help them carry two mountain howitzers up into church steeples. From there they blazed down on street barriers and roof defenders.

By evening it was obvious that the Americans had control of Mexico City. Santa Anna, giving up his last frenzied efforts to save it, withdrew with the remnant of his army.

A mounted band of U. S. dragoons sounded off, horns blaring, kettle drums booming. Behind it on a big bay charger rode Scott in full-dress uniform. Even the Mexican spectators cheered the brave show.

Almost one thousand prisoners were taken, along with large stores of arms and ammunition. The Americans paid a price of 130 killed, 703 wounded, and 29 missing, for the storming of the castle and the city. Santa Anna made one more attempt at resistance. On September 21, commanding 4,000 troops, he circled around to the American base at Puebla, which had been under siege by Mexican guerrillas since September 13. But an American force from Veracruz—commanded by General Joseph Lane—drove him off on October 12, and lifted the siege.

Scott established a model system of military government which kept Mexico under firm control until the country's authorities could reorganize. Nicholas Trist, whom President Polk had sent to Mexico early in 1847 to negotiate a peace treaty with Mexico, was officially recalled to Washington in November, 1847, because of his earlier quarrel with Scott and because the President felt he was offering the Mexicans overly mild peace terms. By this time, however, it was obvious to both Mexicans and Americans that the

Late in the afternoon of September 13, 1847, Worth's soldiers burst through Mexico City's important San Cosme Gate—as shown in the print below—and poured into the city streets.

Mexicans had lost the war, and so both the Mexican government and the British officials in Mexico urged Trist to stay and negotiate further. Risking disgrace at home for disobeying orders Trist remained, and on February 2, 1848, signed the treaty of Guadalupe Hidalgo which included all of Polk's original demands for a peace treaty. It was the decision of both the United States and Mexico to accept the treaty despite the fact that Trist had not leg-

When the Mexican flag flying on the tower of the Castle of Chapultepec (far right) was lowered and the American flag was raised, the thirty remaining members of the ill-fated San Patricio Battalion were hanged from the gallows (far left). The condemned men had nooses placed around their necks and were seated in carts; when the signal was given, the carts were driven out from under them. With their deaths, the history of this band of American deserters was almost over. Although San Patricios may have fought in battles in 1846, their first major contribution to a battle was made at Buena Vista in 1847.

James K. Polk James Buchanan

While President Polk and Secretary of State James Buchanan were in office, the United States boundaries were extended. Buchanan had negotiated the settlement of the Oregon boundary dispute in 1846, and in 1848 Polk and Buchanan helped frame the Treaty of Guadalupe Hidalgo.

ally been the United States representative when he signed it. The treaty was declared in effect on July 4.

By the terms of the treaty, Mexico had to give up two fifths of her territory. She recognized the Rio Grande as the boundary of Texas and ceded California and New Mexico. The California and New Mexico territories, then more than 525,000 square miles, became part of the United States. For them the United States government agreed to pay the sum of $15,000,000 and to forgive the debts Mexico owed the United States.

The end of the Mexican War found the North, still disturbed by the admission to the Union of Texas as a slave state, determined to prevent the new territories gained in the war from being opened to slavery. The balance of power in the United States Senate between slave and free states was still exactly balanced in 1848. The South, however, was deeply concerned over the granting of the status of "free territory" to Oregon. This meant that if the territory of Oregon should one day apply for statehood it would apply as a free state and upset the balance of power. The issue of slavery was so explosive in 1848 that the major parties kept the discussion of it out of their platforms and campaigns. The hero of the Mexican War, General Zachary Taylor, was elected President on the

Whig ticket without ever having taken a stand on slavery.

Taylor was thrown into the midst of the slavery issue, however, sooner than anyone in the government had imagined. In January, 1848, gold was discovered at Sutter's Mill in California. By 1849 thousands of Americans were streaming across country hoping to make their fortunes in the gold fields. Some of the westward-bound settlers stopped in New Mexico and settled there instead of going on to California. President Taylor, an outspoken and strong-willed man, told the Californians and the citizens of New Mexico that they ought to begin to think of statehood and suggested that they draw up constitutions. California did so and chose to be a free state. Although the constitution of New Mexico was not completed until 1850, the

When President John Tyler signed the bill admitting Texas to the Union in 1845, the United States had acquired a vast land area with an uncertain border and an uncertain future. The Mexican War, however, fought during the Polk administration, was concluded with a treaty that added a land area even vaster than Texas to the Union and that finally established most of the United States-Mexican border; the Gadsden Purchase of 1853 established the rest of the border.

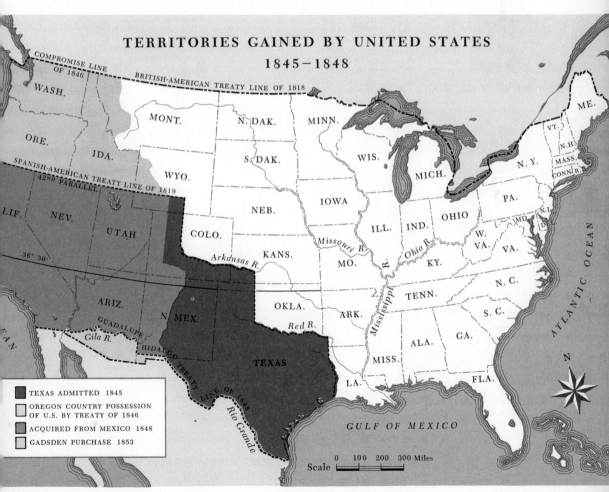

TERRITORIES GAINED BY UNITED STATES
1845–1848

- TEXAS ADMITTED 1845
- OREGON COUNTRY POSSESSION OF U.S. BY TREATY OF 1846
- ACQUIRED FROM MEXICO 1848
- GADSDEN PURCHASE 1853

The nineteenth-century painting at far left shows a Mexican military cadet dressed in the uniform that Los Niños—*the brave young heroes of Chapultepec—wore into the battle.*

A modern Mexican artist has tried to re-create at left the death of Cadet Vincente Suárez, one of the bravest of Los Niños, *who defended his sentry post at the tower stairway of Chapultepec gallantly to the very last.*

General José Mariano Monterde (right) was director of the Mexican Military Academy. in 1847; this was the school Los Niños *attended.*

A modern Mexican painting (below, left) shows the final defense of Chapultepec. The cadets can be seen among the defenders.

sentiment in that territory was against slavery, too. In December, 1849, Taylor asked Congress to admit both California and New Mexico to the Union regardless of their views on slavery. He succeeded in throwing the government into a panic. The South was horrified by the proposal, and the North grew worried because of the intensity of Southern feeling and the danger of a really serious national split over the issue. Congressional leaders, however, immediately went to work on finding a solution or compromise.

It was Henry Clay who finally succeeded in drafting a compromise— known as the Compromise of 1850— which Congress passed after much debate and complex revision. President Taylor died in July, 1850, and so it was his vice president and successor, Millard Fillmore, who signed the compromise legislation in September, 1850. The compromise allowed Calif-

ornia to be admitted to the Union as a free state; New Mexico and Utah would remain territories and were called neither free nor slave territories; the country's fugitive slave laws were strengthened; and the slave trade was abolished in the District of Columbia.

The provisions of the compromise were never popular with extremists in either the North or the South, but the agreement succeeded in delaying a national split between North and South for eleven years. The Civil War, which began in 1861, put an end to the Compromise of 1850 and to all compromise on the issue of slavery in the United States.

In addition to its effect on the slavery question, the Mexican War left two other legacies: a vast amount of valuable territory, and the enmity of many people in Latin America. It is the second legacy that Americans are trying to overcome, even today.

On September 14, 1847, General Winfield Scott (the officer at the head of the colum

...cing right, mounted on a brown horse) rode in triumph into the heart of Mexico City.

Yet, the United States had made it her foreign policy to grant recognition—a precious gift to a young nation—to the Latin American countries as they freed themselves from Spain. And America's Monroe Doctrine had helped prevent the retaking of the new nations by their former rulers. But when the United States entered the Mexican War in 1846 and emerged owning two fifths of Mexico's land area, not only Latin Americans but many men in the United States criticized this nation for having waged the Mexican War.

In his *Memoirs* General Ulysses S. Grant called the Mexican War "the most unjust war" his nation had fought. On the other side of the question, it was argued that the war was fought primarily to protect the rights of the Texans who had become citizens of the United States and were, indeed, menaced by their former Mexican rulers. The important fact is, however, that in the 1840's the United States was a young, growing nation eager to thrust westward to the Pacific. The acquisition by the United States of large amounts of Mexican territory and of Oregon (from the British) represented steps in this westward expansion. Many people began referring to the addition of new land areas to the United States as "Manifest Destiny." The term Manifest Destiny was first used in 1845, in connection with the annexation of Texas. A magazine editor wrote that it was "the fulfillment of our manifest destiny to overspread the continent allotted by Providence for the free development of our yearly multiplying millions." But the idea that it was the destiny of the American people to settle and govern the continent on which they lived went even further back in American history.

In 1801, the year he became President of the United States, Thomas Jefferson wrote: ". . . our rapid multiplication will expand beyond these limits and cover the whole . . . continent with a people speaking the same language, governed in similar forms and by similar laws."

It was inevitable that the trappers and traders, the farmers and land-hungry immigrants living on the edge of the vast, unsettled frontier should move ever westward in search of new land. These people believed in expansion, and they were prepared to fight for it. Frontiersmen had sought the purchase of Louisiana; they had favored the War of 1812 and conquest of Canada; they urged the annexation of Texas and of Oregon; and they were willing to fight Indians or Mexicans or British or anyone else who stood in their path.

Although the war with Mexico was fought largely by and for the westerners, the results benefitted the entire nation. Between them, the Mexican War and the Oregon settlement nearly doubled the land area of the United States, adding 1,200,000 square miles of rich territory, and ensuring that the country would stretch from sea to shining sea.

William H. Richardson, a soldier serving under Doniphan in the Mexican War, included this drawing of "washing day" in an American army camp in the journal he kept of his adventures.

AMERICAN HERITAGE PUBLISHING CO., INC.

BOOK DIVISION

Editor
Richard M. Ketchum

JUNIOR LIBRARY

Editor
Ferdinand N. Monjo

Assistant Editors
Mary Lee Settle • John Ratti

Editorial Assistants
Julia B. Potts • Mary Leverty
Malabar S. Brodeur • Judy Sheftel

Copy Editor
Naomi W. Wolf

Art Director
Emma Landau

Appendix

ACKNOWLEDGMENTS: The editors are deeply grateful to Mr. Joseph Hefter of Mexico City for his time and assistance in researching pictorial material in that country. In addition, they wish expressly to thank the following individuals and organizations for their co-operation and assistance in furnishing material from their collections: Mrs. David W. Knepper, Director, San Jacinto Museum of History Association; Mr. Carl S. Dentzel, Director, Southwest Museum; Lt. Col. John H. Magruder, III, Director, United States Marine Corps Museums; Mr. Edgar M. Howell, Curator, Division of Military History, Smithsonian Institution; Mr. Frederick P. Todd, Director, West Point Museum; Mrs. Paul M. Rhymer, Curator of Prints, Chicago Historical Society; Mr. Detmar H. Finke, Office Chief of Military History, Department of the Army; Mr. Archibald Hanna, Curator, Western Americana Collection, Yale University Library; Mr. Alexander McCook Craighead; Mr. Fernando Lipkau, Mexico, D.F., Photographer; Museum of Churubusco, Mexico, D.F.; and the Museum of History, Chapultepec Castle, Mexico.

PICTURE CREDITS

The source of each picture used in this book is listed below, by page. When two or more pictures appear on one page, they are separated by semicolons. The following abbreviations are used:

AM—The Alamo Museum, San Antonio
CHS—Chicago Historical Society
DA—Office Chief of Military History, Department of the Army
LC—Library of Congress
MC—Museum of Churubusco, Mexico, D.F.

MH—Museum of History, Chapultepec Castle, Mexico
NYHS—Courtesy of the New-York Historical Society, New York City
NYPL—New York Public Library
OPS—Courtesy Harry Shaw Newman, The Old Print Shop, New York City
SJM—San Jacinto Museum of History Association, Texas

SM—Collection Carl S. Dentzel, Southwest Museum, Los Angeles
TMM—Texas Memorial Museum, Austin
TSC—Texas State Capitol, Austin
USMA—United States Military Academy, West Point, New York
YUL—Western Americana Collection, Yale University Library

Maps drawn expressly for this book by David Greenspan

Cover: "Convent of Churubusco," James Walker—DA. **Front End Sheet:** Mexican War Scene, anon.—Kennedy Galleries. **Half Title:** *Davy Crockett's Almanac*. **Title:** SM. **Contents:** *Incidents and Sufferings in the Mexican War*, Lt. G. N. Allen, 1847—YUL. **10** Miguel Gonzalez—Museo Arqueologico Nacional, Madrid. **11** DA. **13** (both) *Costumes civils, militaires et réligieux du Mexique*, Claudio Linati, 1828—NYPL. **15** Freelance Photographers Guild. **16-7** "Mexican Hacienda"—SM. **19** *Bernardo de Gálvez in Louisiana*, J. W. Caughey, © Univ. of California Press, 1934—NYPL. **21** *Mexico y sus Alrededores*—OPS. **24-5** (all) *Costumes civils, op. cit.* **27** (both) *Album Pintoresco de la Republica Mexicana*, Julio Michaud-Thomas, 1848. **28** (both) MH. **30** (l.) MH; (top r.) SJM; (bot. r.) MH. **31** SJM. **32** (both) *Album Pintoresco, op. cit.* **33** Anon.—MH. **34-5** "Proclamation of Iturbide," anon.—MH. **36** (both) LC. **37** (both) CHS. **38** TSC. **40** The John Carter Brown Library, Brown Univ. **41** *Derrotero de la expedicion en la Provincia de Texas*, Antonio de la Pena, Mexico, 1722—Archives of the Indies, Seville. **42** (l.) LC; (cen.) SJM; (r.) AM. **43** AM. **44** Stephen Seymour Thomas—SJM. **45** (l.) William Howard, 1833—TMM; (cen.) AM; (r.) The Alamo. **46** SJM. **47** (l.) *History of Mexico and Its Wars*, John Frost— NYPL; (r.) Library of Congress, Mexico, D.F. **48** *Forget Me Not*, 1846—Texas State Archives. **50** (top) *Life and Times of David G. Burnet*, A. M. Hobby, 1871—NYPL; (bot.) Texas Heritage Foundation, Inc., A. Garland Adair, Ex. Dir. **52-3** Coll. J. B. Arthur, Dallas. **55** Theodore Gentilz—LC. **56** Seth Eastman, 1848—Peabody Museum, Harvard Univ. **57** Daughters of the Republic of Texas Museum, Austin. **58-9** W. G. M. Samuels—Witte Museum, San Antonio. **60** (all) NYHS. **62** (top) TMM; (bot.) TSC. **63** "Battle of San Jacinto," H. A. McCardle—TSC. **64** (l.) *National Portrait Gallery of Americans*, Herring & Longacre, 1867, Vol. 5—NYPL; (r.) Brown Bros. **65** (top) Cook Coll., Valentine Museum; (others) *Los Gobernantes de Mexico*, Manuel Rivera Cambas, 1873, Vol. 2—NYPL. **66-7** "Surrender of Santa Anna," William H. Huddle, *c.* 1900—TSC. **69** *Journal of the Texian Expedition Against Mier*, Thomas J. Green—NYPL. **70** William Garl Browne, *c.* 1846—CHS. **73** *Army Portfolio*, Capt. D. P. Whiting, 1847—NYPL. **74** (both) LC. **75** Eduardo Pingret, 1851—MH. **76** *Major Ringgold's Funeral March*, 1846—YUL. **77** USMA Archives. **78** SJM. **81** (both) SJM. **82** (top l.) *General William Jenkins Worth*, Edward S. Wallace, 1953, © Southern Methodist Univ. Press—NYPL; (top cen.) *Life and Correspondence of John A.*

Quitman, John F. H. Claiborne, 1860, Vol. 1—NYPL; (top r.) National Archives; (bot.) MC. **85** SJM. **86** Missouri Hist. Soc. **86-7** California Hist. Soc. **88-9** John Mix Stanley—Coll. H. J. Lutcher Stark, Courtesy *Life*. **91** (top) Soc. of Calif. Pioneers; (bot.) U. S. Marine Corps Museum. **92-3** (both) *Naval Sketches of the War in California*, William H. Meyers—Franklin D. Roosevelt Library. **94** (l.) *Doniphan's Expedition*, W. E. Connelley, 1907—NYPL; (cen.) NYHS; (r.) CHS. **95** LC. **96** SJM. **98** Coll. H. Armour Smith, *Mathew Brady, Historian With A Camera*, © James D. Horan, Crown Publishers, Inc. **99** (top) Coll. Mrs. Frank J. Coleman; (bot.) CHS. **100** Samuel E. Chamberlain—SJM. **103** LC. **104** OPS. **105** J. M. Rugendas—MH. **106** M. K. Kellogg—NYHS. **108** LC. **109** LC. **112** *The War Between the United States and Mexico . . . Drawings by Carl Nebel*, G. W. Kendall, 1851—NYPL. **115** YUL. **116-17** James Walker—DA. **119** *Incidents and Sufferings in the Mexican War, op. cit.* **120-21** James Walker—DA. **122** (l.) Coll. Lloyd Ostendorf; (cen.) Princeton Univ. Press; (r.) Reproduced from *Pageant of America*, Vol. 6, © Yale University Press. **123** (l.) Coll. Mrs. Frank J. Coleman; (cen.) National Archives; (r.) NYHS. **124-25** "Convent of Churubusco," James Walker—DA. **126** (top) YUL; (bot.) *Battles of the United States*, Henry B. Davison—NYPL. **128-29** G. Escalante—MH. **130** *Lives of General Zachary Taylor and General Winfield Scott*, Arthur Sumpter, 1848—NYPL. **132-33** Kennedy Galleries. **135** LC. **136** James Walker—DA. **137** (cen.) Smithsonian Institution; (bot.) West Point Museum, USMA. **138** MH. **139** LC. **140-41** *My Confession*, Samuel E. Chamberlain—West Point Museum, USMA, Courtesy *Life*. **144** (top l.) H. Military Academy, Mexico, D.F.; (top r.) A. Barrón T., 1957—Assoc. of the H. Military Academy, Mexico, D.F.; (bot.) "The Last Stand at Chapultepec Castle by the Mexican Army, Sept. 13, 1847," A. Barrón T., 1960—Coll. Alexander McCook Craighead. **145** MH. **146-47** *The War Between the United States and Mexico, op. cit.* **149** *Journal of William H. Richardson*, 1848—NYPL. **Back End Sheet:** James Walker, 1854—Coll. Alexander McCook Craighead. **Back Cover:** *History of Mexico and Its Wars*, John Frost—NYPL.

BIBLIOGRAPHY

Bill, Alfred H. *Rehearsal for Conflict.* New York: Alfred A. Knopf, 1947.

Binkley, William C. *The Texas Revolution.* Baton Rouge: Louisiana State University Press, 1952.

Callahan, J. M. *American Foreign Policy in Mexican Relations.* New York: Macmillan, 1932.

Coit, Margaret. *John C. Calhoun.* Boston: Houghton Mifflin, 1950.

Davis, M. E. M. *Under Six Flags, The Story of Texas.* Boston: Ginn, 1897.

DeVoto, Bernard. *Year of Decision.* Boston: Houghton Mifflin, 1950.

Downey, Fairfax. *The Shining Filly.* New York: Schribner's, 1954.

——. "The Tragic Story of the San Patricio Battalion." *American Heritage,* June, 1955.

Henry, Robert. *Story of the Mexican War.* New York: Ungar, 1961.

Horgan, Paul. *The Great River. The Rio Grande.* 2 vols. New York: Rinehart, 1954.

James, Marquis. *The Life of Andrew Jackson.* Indianapolis: Bobbs-Merrill, 1937.

McCoy, Charles. *Polk and the Presidency.* Austin: University of Texas Press, 1960.

Mayer, Brantz. *Mexico: Aztec, Spanish and Republican.* 2 vols. Hartford: S. Drake & Co., 1853.

Mora, Jo. *Californios.* New York: Doubleday, 1949.

Muir, Andrew (ed.). *Texas in 1837.* Austin: University of Texas Press, 1958.

Nadeau, Remi. "Baghdad on the Freeway." *American Heritage,* August, 1958.

Parkes, Henry. *A History of Mexico.* Boston: Houghton Mifflin, 1960.

Reeves, J. S. *American Diplomacy Under Tyler and Polk.* Baltimore: The Johns Hopkins Press, 1907.

Ripley, R. S. *The War with Mexico.* 2 vols. New York: Harper & Bros., 1849.

Rippy, J. F. *The United States and Mexico.* New York: F. S. Crofts, 1931.

Schlesinger, Arthur M. *The Age of Jackson.* Boston: Little, Brown, 1945.

Schmitz, J. W. *Texan Statecraft, 1835-1845.* San Antonio: Naylor Co., 1941.

Sellers, Charles. *James K. Polk, Jacksonian.* Princeton: Princeton University Press, 1957.

Siegel, Stanley. *A Political History of the Texas Republic, 1836-45.* Austin: University of Texas Press, 1956.

Singletary, Otis. *The Mexican War.* Chicago: University of Chicago Press, 1960.

Smith, Justin H. *The Annexation of Texas.* New York: Barnes & Noble, 1941.

——. *The War with Mexico.* 2 vols. New York: Macmillan, 1919.

Spaulding, Oliver L. *The United States Army in War and Peace.* New York: G. P. Putnam, 1937.

Stephenson, N. W. *Texas and the Mexican War.* New Haven: Yale University Press, 1917.

Tinkle, Lon. *13 Days to Glory.* New York: McGraw-Hill, 1958.

Tolbert, Frank X. *The Day of San Jacinto.* New York: McGraw-Hill, 1959.

FOR FURTHER READING

Young readers seeking further information on Texas and the war with Mexico will find the following books to be both helpful and entertaining:

Busoni, Rafaello. *Mexico and the Inca Lands.* New York: Holiday, 1942.

Garst, Shannon. *James Bowie and His Famous Knife.* New York: Messner, 1955.

Hall-Quest, Olga. *Shrine of Liberty: The Alamo.* New York: E. P. Dutton, 1948.

Hoff, Carol. *Wilderness Pioneer:*

Stephen F. Austin of Texas. Chicago: Follett, 1955.

Holbrook, Stewart. *Davy Crockett.* New York: Random House, 1955.

Johnson, William. *Birth of Texas.* Boston: Houghton Mifflin, 1960.

——. *Sam Houston, the Tallest Texan.* New York: Random House, 1953.

Lansing, Marion. *Liberators and*

Heroes of Mexico and Central America. New York: Farrar, Straus & Cudahy, 1941.

Long, Laura. *Fuss 'n' Feathers: a Life of Winfield Scott.* New York: Longmans, Green, 1944.

McNeer, May. *The Mexican Story.* New York: Farrar, Straus & Cudahy, 1953.

October, 1984

Index

Bold face indicates pages on which maps or illustrations appear

Abolitionists, 65
Adams, John Quincy, **36**
Alamo, **half title page,** 37, **40,** 48, 51, **52-53, 54-55, 56,** 57, 60, **111**
American Revolution, 19, 20, 45
Apache Indians, **13,** 18
Arista, Mariano, 72, **75**
Arizona, 8
Atalaya, 108, 113
Augustín I, Emperor, *see* Iturbide, Augustín
Austin, Moses, 39
Austin, Stephen F., **38,** 39, 41-43, **45,** 46, 47, 49, 59, 65
Aztecs, 11, 14
Bancroft, George, 88
Bastrop, Baron de, **38,** 39
Bear Flag, 87, **91**
Benjamin, Calvin, 136
Bent's Fort, 90, **111**
Bishop's Palace (Monterrey), 80, **81,** 83
Black Fort, 80
Boca del Rio, 79
Bonaparte, Joseph, 20-21
Bonaparte, Napoleon, 12, 20, 43
Bonham, James Butler, 54, 57
Borginnis, Sarah, **9**
Bosque de Santiago, **81**
Bowie, James (Jim), **45,** 46, 47, 51, 54, 55-56, 57
Bowie knife, 46, 56, 57, 63
Bragg, Braxton, 84, 97, **99,** 101, 102
Brown, Jacob, **9**
Buchanan, James, **142**
Buena Vista, Battle of, **title page,** 95, **96-103, 111,** 122, 123, 141
Burleson, Edward, 46, 49
Burnet, David G., **50,** 57
Bustamante, Anastasio, 31, 42, 47
Calhoun, John C., **60**
California, 8, 12, 37, 68, 69, 71, 86-95
  ceded to U. S., 142
  gold rush, 143
  Republic of, 88
  settlement of, 12, 22, 37
  threatened by Russia, 12, 22
Calleja del Rey, Félix María, 33
Canada, 12
Canalizo, Valentín, 109
Carson, Kit, 90
Casas, Fra Bartolomé de las, 14
Cerro Gordo, 108, **111, 112-15**
Chapultepec, 8, **110, 132**-38, **144**
Cherokee Indians, 46

Churubusco, **cover,** 110, 123, **124-31**
Civil War, U. S., 8, 39
Clay, Henry, **60,** 65, 68, 145
Colorado, 8
Comanche Indians, 18, 45
Compromise of 1850, 145
Contreras, Battle of, **120-23**
Copano, 43
Córdoba, Treaty of, 26
Corpus Christi, Texas, 69, **111**
Cortés, Hernando, **10,** 11
Cos, Martín, 33, 43, **47,** 49
Cowboys, 14
Creoles (*criollos*), 14, **20-21,** 22, **24, 25,** 36, 37
Crockett, Davy, **half title page,** 45, 46, 51, **52,** 54, 56, 57
Dallas, George, 64
Dallas, Texas, 64
Davis, Jefferson, 83, 101, **123**
"Deguello," 54, 56
Dickinson, Almaron, 54, 57
Dickinson, Sue, 54, 56, **57**
Dolores, Mexico, 22
Doniphan, Alexander W., 90, 91, 92, **94, 95, 111**
Drum, Simon, 122-23, 136
Duncan James, 74
El Brazito, Texas, 91, **111**
Eldorado, 12
El Paso, Texas, 91, **111**
Encomienda system, 13
Fannin, James Walker, 46, 47, 51, 54, 59, 60, 61, 73
Ferdinand VII, King of Spain, 20-21, 26
Fernández, Manuel Félix (Guadalupe Victoria), 29, **30**
Fillmore, Millard, 145
Florida, 12, 41, 71
Fort Brown, **9,** 71, 72, **111**
France, Louisiana and, 12, 20
Franciscans, 14
Frémont, John Charles, 87, **95**
French and Indian War, 12
Gachupines, 14, 22, 25
Gadsden Purchase, **143**
Galveston, Texas, 20
Gálvez, Bernardo de, **19,** 20
Goliad (La Bahia), Texas, 37, 46-47, 51, 54, 59, 60, 61, **111**
Gonzales, Texas, 33, 45, 54, **111**
Grant, James, 50
Grant, Ulysses S., 8, 83, 84, **122,** 138, 148
Guadalajara, Mexico, 22
Guadalupe Hidalgo, treaty of, 140, 142, 143

Guadalupe Victoria, *see* Fernández, Manuel Félix
Guanajuato, Mexico, 22
Guerrero, Vicente, 29, 31
Haciendas, 14, **16-17,** 18-19
Harney, William S., 114
Herrera, José, 64, **65**
Hidalgo y Costilla, Father, 22, 26, **27,** 29, **31,** 33
Houston, Sam, **42,** 43, **44,** 46, 51, 59, 61, 63-64, 65, **66-67,** 68
Independence Day, Mexican, 22
Indians, 12, 14, 18-20, 36, 42
  Apache, **13,** 18
  Aztec, 11, 14
  Cherokee, 46
  Comanche, 18, 45
  conversion to Christianity, 13, 14
  Kiowa, 18
  Mayan, 14
  Seminole, 8, 71
  slavery and, 13, 14
  Tejas, 12
Iturbide, Agustín, 26, 29, **30, 35,** 46
Jackson, Andrew, **36,** 44, 64, 65, 68
Jackson, Thomas J. ("Stonewall"), 8, **123,** 135-36, 138
Jalapa, Mexico, **111,** 115, 117
Jefferson, Thomas, 12, 148
Jesuits, 14
Johnston, Albert Sidney, 8, 83
Johnston, Joseph E., 8
Kearny, Phil, 130-31
Kearny, Stephen Watts, 71, **86,** 88, 89, 90, 95, **110-11**
Kiowa Indians, 18
Lamar, Mirabeau, 68
La Mesa, **92-93**
Lane, Joseph, 139
La Salle, Rene Robert, 12
Las Vegas, New Mexico, 90, **111**
Lee, Robert E., 8, 105-106, 108-109, 113, 119-21, 122, **123**
Lone Star flag, 46, **62**
Longstreet, James, 138
Louisiana Purchase, 12, 41, 148
Louisiana territory, 12, 20, 22, 23
Lovejoy, Elijah, 65
Magruder, John Bankhead, 135-36
Maine, 65
Manifest Destiny, 69, 148
Martínez, Antonio, 39
Matamoros, Mexico, 50-51, 59, 71, 72, **111**

152

May, Charles, **74, 77**
Mayan Indians, 14
Mazatlán, 110, **111**
McClellan, George B., **122**
Meade, George Gordon, 8, 83, **122**
Mestizos, 14, 22
Mexican War, 69, 71-148
Mexico,
  as Spanish province, 12
  dictatorship, 31, 33, 36, 43
  independence, 21-22, 25, 26, 36
  invaded by Spain, 11
  monarchy, 26, 29
  republic established, 29
  slavery in, 29, 42
Mexico City, Mexico, **20-21,** 22, **34-35,** 68, 71, 94, 107, 110, **111,** 119, 125, 131, 132, 138-39, **146-47, back end sheet**
Mier y Teran, 42
Milam, Benjamin, **42,** 43, 46-47, 49
Missions and missionaries, 12, 14, **15,** 37, 51
Missouri, 39, 65
Missouri Compromise, 39, 65
Molino del Rey, 110, **128-29,** 133-34
Monroe Doctrine, 148
Monterde, José Mariano, **145**
Monterey, California, 89, 90, **91, 110**
Monterrey, Mexico, 71, 79, 80, **81, 82,** 83, **84-85,** 87, 94, 95, **111**
Montezuma, 11-12, 132
Morelos, Father José, 22, 26, 29, **32, 33**
Napoleon, *see* Bonaparte
Negroes, 14, **24,** 36
Neill, J. C., 51
Nevada, 8
New Mexico, 8, 12, 68, 69, 87, 91, 95, 143
  ceded to U. S., 142
  colonized, 12
New Orleans, 20, 39, 45, 50
Niños, Los, 8, 138, **144**
O'Brien, John Paul Jones, 100-101, 122, 123
O'Donojú, Juan, 26
Old Whitey (Taylor's horse), **title page,** 11, **70,** 72, **74,** 76, **96,** 99
Oregon territory, 68, 142, **143,** 148
Our Lady of Guadalupe, 29
Padierna, *see* Contreras, Battle of
Palo Alto, Battle of, **front end sheet,** 73-75, 78, 94, **111**
Paredes, Mariano, 64, **65**
Pedraza, Manuel Gómez, 29, 31
Pedregal, the, 120-21, 122

Perry, Matthew, C., 106
Pickett, George, 138
Pierce, Franklin, 118
Pillow, Gideon, **121,** 122
Plan de Iguala, 26
Point Isabel, 72, 79, **111**
Polk, James K., **64,** 68, 69, 78, 87, 94, 95, 118, 139, 140, **142,** 143
Puebla, Mexico, 118, 119, 139
Quitman, John A., **82, 111,** 134, 138
Raton Pass, 90
Refugio, Texas, 59, **111**
Resaca de la Palma, Battle of, **front end sheet, 74,** 76, **77,** 78, 94, **111**
Ridgely, Randolph, 76
Riley, John, 80, 84, 126, 127, 130, 131
Ringgold, Samuel, 73, 75, **76**
Russia, California threatened by, 12, 22
Sacramento, Battle of, 92, **110**
Salado, Mexico, **69, 111**
Saltillo, Mexico, 97, 98, **111**
San Antonio, Texas, 33, 37, **40, 41,** 46, 47, **48-49,** 50-51, 54, 57, **58-59,** 71, **78-79, 111**
San Antonio River, 46
San Cosme Gate (Mexico City), 138, **139, back end sheet**
San Diego, California, 89, 90, **110**
San Felipe, 49, 51, **111**
San Gabriel, Battle of, 90-91, **110**
San Jacinto, Battle of, 61, **62-63,** 64, 65, **66-67, 111**
San Jacinto River, 61
San José, mission of, **15**
San Juan de Ulúa, **102-103**
San Pasqual, California, 90, **110**
San Patricio, Texas, 59, 60, **111**
San Patricio Battalion, 79-80, 126-27, 130, 131, 138, **140,** 141
Santa Anna, Antonio López de, 29, **30,** 31, 33, 36, 43, **46,** 47, 50, 51, 54-57, 59, 61, 63-68, 95, 97-98, 100, 102-103, 107-108, **109,** 113-15, 118, 119, 122, 125-27, 130-32, 139
Santa Fe, New Mexico, 71, 88, 89, 90, 91, 95, **111**
Scott, Winfield, 71, 94-95, 103-108, 110-19, 122, 123, 125-27, 132-34, 138, 139, **146**
Seminole Indians, war with the, 8, 71
Semmes, Raphael, 138
Serra, Fra Junípero, 14
Seven Cities of Cibola, 12
Sherman, Thomas W., 101
Shields, James, 114
Siete Leyes (Seven Laws), 33

Slavery, 13, 14, 29, 39, 42, 65
Slidell, John, 64, **65,** 69
Sloat, John D., 88-89, 90, 91, **94,** 95, 110
Smith, Erastus (Deaf), **42,** 43, 46, 49, 61, **66-67**
Smith, Justin, quoted, 98
Smith, Persifor, 122
Sonoma, California, **86-87,** 91, **110**
Spain,
  Florida sold by, 41
  Louisiana and, 12, 22
  territory in America, 12, 14, **23**
Spy Company, 127, 130
Stockton, Robert F., 89, 90, **94,** 95
Suarez, Vincente, **144**
Tampico, Mexico, 29, 71, 95, **111**
Taylor, Zachary, **title page,** 8, 11, 69, **70-80,** 83, 84, 87, 94, 95, **96,** 97 99-103, 110, **111,** 142-43, 145
Tejas Indians, 12
Texas,
  annexation of, 8, 36, 60, 64, 65, 68, 69, 142, 143, 148
  independence declared, 50, 57
  Republic of, 64-68
  settlement of, 12, 22, 37, 39-42, 66
  slavery in, 29, 42, 65, 142
  war for independence, 43, 45-65
Texas Rangers, 11, 71, **85**
Thomas, George H., 8
Travis, William, **42,** 46, 51, 54, 55, 56, 57
Treaty of Córdoba, 26
Trist, Nicholas P., 118, 139, 140
Twiggs, Daniel E., 113-14
Tyler, John, 36, **37,** 68, 69, 143
Ugartechia, Colonel, 45
Urrea, José, 59-61
Utah, 8, 145
Valencia, Gabriel, 121
Van Buren, Martin, 36, **37,** 65, 68
Vaqueros (cowboys), 14, 18
Veracruz, Mexico, 64, 71, 94, 95, **102-103,** 104-107, **108-109, 111,** 118
Wallace, Lew, 102
Walnut Springs, **81**
War of 1812, 8, 45, 46
Washington-on-Brazos, Texas, 50, 57
Webster, Daniel, **60**
Wool, John Ellis, 71, **78, 82,** 97, **98,** 100, 110, **111**
Worth, William Jenkins, 80, **82,** 83, 84, 138, 139, **back end sheet**
Wyoming, 8
Zambos, 14

153